85-1189

P9-CJR-552

THE PREDICAMENT OF HUMAN RIGHTS

The Carter and Reagan Policies, Volume V

Nicolai N. Petro

With a preface and introduction by

Kenneth W. Thompson

WITHDRAWN

UNIVERSITY
PRESS OF
AMERICA

Shambaugh Library

LANHAM • NEW YORK • LONDON

JC
571
.P49
X

AMERICAN VALUES PROJECTED ABROAD

A SERIES FUNDED BY THE EXXON EDUCATION FOUNDATION

Copyright © 1983 by

University Press of America,™ Inc.

4720 Boston Way
Lanham, MD 20706

3 Henrietta Street
London WC2E 8LU England

All rights reserved

Printed in the United States of America

Library of Congress Cataloging in Publication Data

Petro, Nicolai N.
    The predicament of human rights.

    (American values projected abroad ; v. 5)
    Bibliography: p.
    1. United States–Foreign relations–1977–1981. 2.
United States–Foreign relations–1981–   . 3. Civil
rights–United States. 4. Civil rights. I. Title. II. Series.
JX1417.A74   1982 vol. 5 303.4'8273s   83–10448
ISBN 0–8191–3325–6   327.73
ISBN 0–8191–3326–4 (pbk.)

Co-published by arrangement with
The White Burkett Miller Center of Public Affairs
University of Virginia

As with all first books,
this one must be dedicated, lovingly,
to my mother and father.
Thank you for all the years of
love, support, and guidance.

Acknowledgments

I would like to express my gratitude to the Miller Center of Public Affairs, to the Exxon Education Foundation and to the professors who read and commented on portions of this manuscript: David Little, Donald F. Kettl, Whittle Johnston, and especially, Kenneth W. Thompson, without whose support and encouragement this work could not have been completed.

Thanks also to Barbara Teague for her support and criticism at key stages of my work.

Whereas the credit for any merit of this volume is widely shared, I alone am responsible for its faults.

TABLE OF CONTENTS

PREFACE

Kenneth W. Thompson

Nicolai Petro is a young scholar whose background and interests make him singularly well-qualified to write on human rights. His background is Russian and German. Many of his relatives remain east of what Winston S. Churchill called the Iron Curtain. As a young man, Mr. Petro has travelled throughout Europe and observed the workings of regimes in both east and west. He has command of six languages and a wide ranging-knowledge of European and Russian history.

Mr. Petro pursued undergraduate studies at the University of Virginia in both foreign affairs and history, receiving a *summa cum laude* in history for his honors thesis on dissent in the USSR. He has maintained the highest standards in graduate studies in the Woodrow Wilson Department of Government and Foreign Affairs, earned the certificate in Russian and East European Studies, and currently teaches comparative government at Sweet Briar College. He was the editor of an interdisciplinary journal, *Thoughtlines*, created by Professor Dante Germino and his colleagues as an outgrowth of a program on social values funded by the National Endowment of the Humanities. He has held the Richard M. Weaver, DuPont, Helen E. Lassen, Institute for the Study of World Politics and Earhart Fellowships. At a time when most graduate students concentrate exclusively on their studies, Mr. Petro has published several important articles and has begun to establish himself as a serious contributor to the literature of international relations.

In the present volume, Mr. Petro demonstrates his continued intellectual growth and development. He achieves a measure of objectivity and detachment that is always difficult with subjects on which emotions run high. Furthermore, Mr. Petro has researched the ways in which the Carter and Reagan administrations have sought to implement their differing approaches to human rights. Few if any authorities have written on the policy-making process in human rights under Presidents Carter and Reagan. For this reason, Mr. Petro's inquiry is a work of original scholarship and considerable value. We are pleased to publish this study as the fourth volume in a series made possible, by the Exxon Educational Foundation. The series is devoted to an overall review of American values projected abroad, a process in which human rights have played an increasingly important part in recent years.

INTRODUCTION

Kenneth W. Thompson

No single study of human rights will have the last word on the subject. The issues that are raised are deeply contentious and divisive. The champions and the critics of human rights policy range themselves along an intellectual and political battlefield directing volleys of fire against one another. Yet the subject is fraught with consequences for sound foreign policy and the maintenance of world peace. We need discussions that seek to clarify both the normative basis of human rights and the prospects for peaceful and constructive change among nations.

It would be unthinkable in a series on American values to neglect the discussion of human rights. The American experience and the lessons to be drawn from the political experiences of "a city on the hill" dedicated to the pursuit of fundamental freedoms and human rights are too important to be left to the apologists and the cynics. Human rights are not the sum total of American values but neither are they a matter to be ignored or passed over. On human rights as on the other great issues of American politics and foreign policy, serious thinkers must, with William James, "make an unusually stubborn attempt to think clearly." Neither moralism nor cynicism provide a sound basis for thinking about human rights. Practical morality is a more effective and legitimate approach to the problem.

Practical morality seeks to relate what is morally desirable with what is politically possible. It is an ancient tradition which calls on the resources of moral reasoning. According to this tradition, values compete and conflict with one another. The Supreme Court has decreed that freedom of speech and press doesn't give persons the right "to cry fire in a crowded theater." Freedom and order compete with one another. Peace and justice may be in tension. The dictates of

3

economic growth must be balanced against protection of the environment; controlling inflation is a goal that policymakers can follow only as they seek to hold down unemployment. Human rights in turn must be advanced in accordance with the demands of national security. No single goal is an absolute in foreign policy. Each must be seen as it affects other valid national purposes.

Moreover, no single nation can determine the goals and policies of another sovereign state. We live in a world of independent nation states each with its own history, political traditions and national interests. To bring about fundamental changes in the approach to human rights in other sovereign states requires fundamental changes in traditions and political systems. Even international organizations are limited in the influence they exert within the territorial boundaries of member states. Such limits are greater for a single nation state, even the most powerful, seeking to work its will within other nation states. Nations tend to overestimate the extent of their national fiat in the international community.

Yet prudence makes possible more limited changes. The influence of ideas is incremental; respect for law in western countries goes back to Roman law, the Napoleonic code and the common law. In developing countries, colonial regimes planted the seeds of the rule of law which merged with native traditions of law and order. In various parts of the world, nations are making their way toward more dependable and predictable systems of social control and human rights.

A first step in the understanding of the implementation of human rights is a better understanding of policymaking in the United States from 1977 to the present. The lessons to be learned from this relatively brief period in our history may better prepare Americans for the next challenge. It is easier to proclaim a worthy social and political goal than to pursue it through the complex maze of decision making. It is surprising that so few scholars have devoted their best efforts to understanding what Petro calls the human rights predicament. We know all too little about the difficult choices faced in molding a human rights policy in the Carter and Reagan administrations.

The aim of this short volume is to inspire others to continue the inquiry which Nicolai Petro has begun. If his study serves no other purpose than to stimulate further study, it will have been worth a young scholar's efforts.

HUMAN RIGHTS AND THE TRADITIONS OF AMERICAN DIPLOMACY

The term "human rights" has become almost synonymous with the Carter administration. For many at home and abroad it symbolized that administration, setting it apart from previous administrations presumably unconcerned with human rights. For others, the policy was the equivalent of "moral imperialism," subverting the tempered self-interest that had traditionally guided American foreign policy. The question of what role human rights have played in this nation's history lies at the root of much of the recent debate over human rights.

President Carter and his supporters held the view that the "U.S. government frequently defended individual freedom, self-determination and civil liberties in statements by various presidents declaring their global concern for liberty,"[1] citing documents like Thomas Jefferson's letter to James Madison in 1782 in which Jefferson wrote that "a bill of rights is what the people are entitled to against every government on earth."[2] Although students of that period now agree that Jefferson was thinking only of the nations of Europe and North America,[3] he is often listed among those Presidents, including William McKinley, Woodrow Wilson, Franklin D. Roosevelt, John F. Kennedy and even Lyndon Johnson, who verbally espoused human rights as a foreign policy concern. Advocates for a vigorous human rights policy argue along with Tom Farer that: "From the Revolutionary War of Independence to this day, concern for human rights has been a prominent theme in the rhetoric of American foreign policy."[4]

Those who argue for a more moderate role for human rights point out, however, that our rhetoric has usually diverged from the actual conduct of our foreign policy. In his classic study of the foreign policy of the Founding Fathers, Paul A. Varg argues that this dichotomy has been present since the birth of our nation. American nationalism derived great benefit from early American idealism. It strengthened the new republic's sense of separate identity, of being free from special privilege, aristocracy and the arbitrary intrigues of foreign courts. "Americans prided themselves on being the model republican society that the rest of the world could emulate."[5] Being the only republican power of that period, and still healing from the wounds of separation from Great Britain, however, we could offer a corrupt world little more than verbal support. Our weakness and isolation counseled prudence in projecting our ideals beyond our shores.

At no time was this reality more evident than during President Washington's traumatic refusal to commit troops to the cause of the French Revolution, despite our obligation under treaty of friendship to do so. In 1821, John Quincy Adams gave this non-assertive, self-interested foreign policy stance its most eloquent expression:

> Wherever the standard of freedom and independence has been or shall be unfurled, here shall be America's heart, her bene-dictions, and her prayers. But she goes not abroad in search of monsters to destroy. She is the well-wisher to the freedom and independence of all. She is the champion and vindicator of her own. She will recommend the general cause by the countenance of her voice, and by the benignant sympathy of her example. . . . [If she did more] she might become the dictatress of the world. She would no longer be the ruler of her own spirit.

Throughout the 19th century, then, "declarations notwith-standing, morality enjoyed ephemeral fashion in U.S. foreign policy,"[7] and played only a marginal role in the pursuit of our national commercial interests.[8] Given the nation's disinterest in foreign affairs during most of this period, non-interventionism rather than human rights was the main determinant of American conduct abroad. The American view of natural rights, according to Professor M. Glenn Johnson, put the right of non-intervention in another state's internal affairs first.[9]

Woodrow Wilson was the first president to seriously challenge the traditional non-interventionism of American foreign policy and institutionalize the notion that America's unique experiment with freedom fully justified intervention in the affairs of other states.

Wilson anticipated the day , when "America will come into the full light of day when all shall know that she puts human rights above all other rights, and that her flag is the flag not only of America but of humanity."[10]

Some diplomatic historians, however, have indicated that Wilson espoused human rights in a much narrower sense than we seek them today. Wilson did not, for example, embrace the Japanese sponsored issue of racial equality, nor did he apply the principle of self-determination to the peoples of the victorious empires.[11]

Along with a strong preference for democratic institutions, Wilson stressed the need for peaceful change in the world. He believed that if given the ability to choose, the people would always make the correct choices. This faith in the inevitable triumph of democracy was soon shattered though, first by the Bolshevik coup d'etat of November 1917 and later by the rise of Adolf Hitler in Germany.

By 1940, President Roosevelt perceived the need to expand our definition of human rights and anchor self-determination more firmly to other universally recognized rights than Wilson had done. According to Willard Range, "the President reaffirmed the right of people to choose their own form of government; but then he qualified that right by declaring that such choice should be predicated on certain freedoms which he thought were essential everywhere. 'We know,' he [Roosevelt] went on, 'that we ourselves shall never be wholly safe at home unless other governments recognize such freedoms.' "[12] In order to ensure a lasting world peace, therefore, beginning with his "Four Freedoms" address to Congress in 1941, Roosevelt gradually revised the presumption of a nation's internal inviolability in favor of a modified principle that would justify Great Power intervention (later United Nations intervention) to rectify the more egregious human rights violations that could conceivably lead to conflict among states.[13]

After World War II, for the first time in American diplomacy, the security of the United States was linked to internal conditions in foreign nations, and the United States was in an excellent position to influence these conditions. Amidst the rubble and ashes America had survived relatively untarnished and comparatively stronger than before she had entered the war.

While she proceeded to shape her former enemies (and many of her allies) both economically and politically, one stumbling block remained from the time of Wilson—Soviet Communism. While Hitler had been defeated, Stalin remained at the helm of the Soviet ship of state, and efforts to strengthen his sense of common interest

7

with the Western Allies had begun to crumble even during the war. Prior to 1935, Russia's internal turmoil had greatly diminished the threat she posed internationally, so that anti-Communism was a relatively insignificant part of U.S. diplomacy. Presidents and secretaries of state after Roosevelt, however, soon saw Communism as the gravest threat to liberty and peace in the world, and in their minds the objectives of human rights and self-determination became almost synonymous with anti-Communism.[14]

The rapid escalation of tensions through the 1950's and 60's into a "cold war" caused the anti-Communist motivation behind our policies to supercede our human rights efforts in visibility and significance, eventually leaving them so far behind that contemporary observers have trouble discerning any idealistic component to our post-war containment policy. Townsend Hoopes, author of *The Devil and John Foster Dulles*, typically sees the standard of our post-war foreign policy solely in terms of anti-Communism:

> I faced . . . the dawning realization that an era in American foreign policy had ended—an era of more than 20 years' duration in which the American people had found a large measure of their political *raison d'etre* as well as much moral comfort, in fusing their perception of national interest with what seemed an unarguable ideological imperative: namely, the absolute need to confront (or at least oppose) every manifestation of communism at every point on the globe.[15]

In fact, though, our post-war policy remained greatly concerned with the rights of other nations and individuals. Arguably, it was the thrust of this idealism, unmatched by either a willingness or capability to realize our ideals, that led in later years to the widespread domestic perception of our foreign policy as weak and indecisive.

President Nixon entered office in 1969 keenly aware of the nation's isolationist mood and desire to limit its obligations abroad. He and his national security adviser Henry Kissinger worked steadily to decrease United State involvement abroad and redefine its mission in a manner which the American public, sickened by the Vietnam debacle, would find acceptable. While sharing many of the same objectives as his opponents, who viewed the failure of containment as stemming from the *lack* of commitment to a morally defensible ideal (e.g., human rights), Kissinger saw the failure of American post-war policy as the result of overcommitting American resources and argued that human rights must not become a "vocal objective" of foreign policy. In his confirmation hearings, Kissinger stated before Congress, "I believe it is dangerous for us to make the domestic policy of countries around the world a direct objective of American foreign policy."[17]

During his tenure as Secretary of State, Kissinger consequently opposed all congressional attempts to "interfere" in his conduct of foreign policy. In 1975 he embargoed a report on the human rights records of aid recipient countries requested by Congress on the grounds that "neither U.S. security interests nor human rights cause could be served" by such "public obloquy."[18] Patrick Breslin believes the State Department under Kissinger was seeking "to keep Congress in the dark about human rights violations by regimes receiving U.S. aid . . . State often appeared before Congress as an apologist for the abuses of dictators. . . . State seemed generally more defensive about a nation's human rights record the more the United States was associated with its regime."[19]

For human rights activists who viewed the decline in American leadership as the result of a failure to espouse high moral standards, Kissinger's solution of linking Soviet interests to ours through a network of expanding agreements (détente) did not resolve this problem. Indeed, for them any foreign policy which did not address the domestic necessity of reasserting fundamental American values was doomed to failure.

As the 1976 elections drew closer Kissinger seemed to give greater consideration to the domestic component of American foreign policy, but for many his views were already discredited.

CONGRESS AND HUMAN RIGHTS

Given our country's preoccupation with the morality of international affairs, there has always been some role for human rights to play in our foreign policy. Under Nixon and Kissinger the pursuit of human rights was considered detrimental to our vital interests and was thus, whenever possible, ignored. It was the executive branch's interest in promoting human rights under President Carter, more than the strengthened congressional legislation, that finally made people take notice of the new policy. The credit for adopting human rights as a policy objective cannot, however, go entirely to the President and his advisers. Long before Carter entered office in January 1977 the Congress had enacted the legislative requirements that formed the backbone of the human rights policy.

Congressional dissatisfaction with the executive branch's conduct of foreign affairs, specifically with its lack of concern for human rights, reached a high point during the early seventies. At that time several disparate interest groups joined to express their common concern for human rights. Congressman Donald Fraser, then head of the House Subcommittee on International Affairs, cites three concerns that united human rights activists: the easing of Cold War tensions, the changing perception of America's role in the world after Vietnam, and the feeling that the United States had in many ways directly abetted human rights violations by upholding repressive regimes.[20] In a similar vein Mark Schneider, later Deputy Assistant Secretary of State for Human Rights under Carter, asserts that the main reasons for the burning concern with human in the 1970's were: (1) the domestic civil rights movement, which "educated vast numbers of Americans . . . in the denial of basic rights"; (2) Watergate, which awoke public awareness that government could itself "impinge on the rights of American citizens," and yet could be successfully thwarted by a "combination of a free press, an independent judiciary, and an aroused public opinion"; (3) Vietnam, which Schneider claims "represented an abdication of moral leadership and a denial of past values. There was a vague notion that somehow the United States was preventing the self-determination of others."[21]

Congressional activism with regard to Vietnam at times led to direct conflict with the executive branch. "One sees the same names pressing for an end to U.S. involvement who later raised critical objections about the absence of sufficient weight to human rights concerns," Schneider argues. "In the Senate, these critics included Senators Mansfield, Church, John Sherman Cooper, Clifford Case, Kennedy, Brooke, McGovern, Abzug, Ryan and Burton."[22] The conflict over Vietnam led these congressmen to several conclusions which endured beyond the end of the war: first, the dilemma of a foreign policy "in conflict with basic human values"; second, "the near impossibility in a democratic society of conducting, over a long period of time, a foreign policy against the opposition of a substantial segment of the people"; and third, "the willingness of Congress to reassert its role in determining the direction of U.S. foreign policy and . . . be more responsive to popular opinion."[23]

The divisiveness of the Vietnam debate, the criticisms of powerful congressmen and senators—like Edward Kennedy, Chairman of the Senate Refugee Subcommittee, who denounced the exclusion of human rights considerations from détente—,[24] and Watergate, all led to growing Congressional assertiveness in foreign policy. There was, in the words of one observer, a growing sense in the Congress that a "breach had opened between American values and American foreign policy."[25]

On this issue the mood of the Congress seemed to coincide remarkably with the mood of the nation. By 1976 over half the nation's legislators had been at their jobs less than two years. Very few congressmen in office during the early sixties still remained.[26] Those newly elected had "loose party ties and little personal loyalty to the President. They exhibit pronounced skepticism about traditional political initiations and toward those who advocate a 'responsible' approach to foreign policy (read: toeing old lines of bipartisanship and seniority)."[27] This gathering of inexperienced elected officials dissatisfied with the state of our foreign policy and wanting quick results led to improbable coalitions in support of human rights initiatives. Liberals, who were more inclined to feel strongly about human rights and the need to reduce "immoral" arms transfers, joined forces with conservatives, who saw human rights as a means of reducing spending on multilateral and bilateral assistance.[28]

Congress' backlash against Henry Kissinger's *Realpolitik* found further expression in the Fraser Subcommittee hearing on human rights entitled, "Human Rights in the World Community: A Call for U.S. Leadership." The report concluded that "the human rights factor is not accorded the high priority it deserved in our country's foreign policy" and that "too often it becomes invisible on the vast foreign policy horizon. . . ."[29] The report found the administration's record to date "random," and "unpredictable," and came up with a list of recommendations for improving U.S. responsiveness to human rights considerations. "A higher priority for human rights," the Fraser report concludes, "is both morally imperative and practically necessary."[30] According to Sandra Vogelgesang, later an administration human rights official, these reports "were a conscious effort to educate Capitol Hill, the executive branch, and the country on human rights."[31]

The heightened interest in human rights soon bore its first legislative fruits. In 1973, Senator Kennedy introduced an amendment expressing concern for human rights in Chile.[32] The first congressional policy statement was inserted as Section 32 of the Foreign Assistance Act of 1973:

> It is the sense of Congress that the President should deny any economic or military assistance to the government of any foreign country which practices the internment or imprisonment of that country's citizens for political purposes.[33]

The Foreign Assistance Act of 1973 also set forth the "New Directions" concept in bilateral assistance, away from large capital transfers to food production, nutrition, rural development, population planning, health, education, and resource development. The new policy on foreign assistance thus dovetailed nicely with the policy on aid transfers.[34]

In 1974, dissatisfied with Kissinger's refusal to comply with the "sense of Congress" resolution passed a year earlier, Congress amended the International Development and Food Assistance Act to specifically *prohibit* the use of funds to aid any government "which engages in a consistent pattern of gross violations of internationally recognized human rights . . . unless such assistance will directly benefit the needy." This amendment, known through its sponsor as the Harkin Amendment, also required the State Department to demonstrate that aid would indeed reach the needy and further required the President to submit an annual report to Congress on his compliance with the requirements of the new legislature.

By late 1976, congressional initiatives had thus forced the State

Department into consultations with Capitol Hill on human rights issues despite Kissinger's original attempts to dismiss the policy as inappropriate.[35] With the new congressional laws on human rights the burden of proof for the continuance or initiation of a policy shifted from the Congress to the administration.

Meanwhile, the Democratic contender for the presidency, James Earl Carter, was campaigning vigorously against the lack of moral leadership in the White House, citing human rights as the clearest example of this. The best palliative to the nation's recent problems, Carter implied, would be his own combination of strong religious convictions, civil rights activism, and rational, businesslike administration.[36]

For Carter, human rights was the issue which, better than any other, could re-build the domestic consensus and create an American role in the world which, in the words of his running-mate Walter Mondale, would leave the American people "feeling good." The issue was also smart politics, as the leaders of Congress had already discovered. It would permit the President to reassert American leadership abroad without either a heavy monetary expenditure or an intricate and taxing foreign policy program.[37] The electoral appeal of human rights thus appears to have been a major factor in embracing it. All the other Democratic contenders endorsed it; according to one Carter aide, "human rights was an issue which you could bracket Kissinger and Ford on both sides."[38]

After a campaign so heavily based on the appeal of human rights, its adoption as a key component of the President's new foreign policy became a virtual necessity.[39] In a speech on morality in foreign policy at the University of Notre Dame, therefore, President Carter reaffirmed that human rights were the "soul" of our foreign policy. Later he vowed, as he would on numerous other occasions, that "as long as I am President, the government of the United States will continue, throughout the world, to enhance human rights. No force on earth can separate us from that commitment."[40]

Despite his firm personal commitment to human rights, the President soon found himself at odds with the 95th Congress. No sooner did he enter office than the Congress tried to extend Harkin language to the Inter-American Development Bank and the African Development Bank. Ignoring his campaign rhetoric, the President fought hard to prevent these additions. In a letter to Speaker of the House Tip O'Neill, Secretary of State Vance complained that restrictions on U.S. participation in the international financial institutions would interfere with diplomatic attempts to improve human rights practices in some countries.[41]

Prior to the new administration, Congress had passed legislation prohibiting foreign assistance transfers to governments violating human rights and had singled out individual countries for embargoes. The new President, however, vowed to go beyond these merely punitive policies and to use his influence to improve human rights conditions around the world.[42] "Our aim," according to Assistant Secretary of State for Human Rights Patricia Derian, "is neither confrontation nor conflict, but encouragement of improvement in human rights practices. One way to do this is to demonstrate that there are costs to violators and benefits to those who respect human rights."[43]

The new administration sought to advance three categories of rights: freedom from government infringement upon personal integrity; the fulfillment of basic human needs; and the right to civil and political liberties.[44] The pursuit of these objectives, spokesmen for the administration often repeated, serves to link our foreign policy to the "broad channel of our domestic values,"[45] and also to "restore public consensus behind U.S. foreign policy in general and détente in particular."[46] Moreover, the administration argued that the pursuit of human rights was an obligation under the United Nations Charter.[47]

Secretary of State Vance discussed the new policy guidelines in his testimony before Congress on March 2, 1977:

> Our concern for human rights must be considered together with other economic and security goals. We believe that in some instances, these judgements can be arrived at on a country-by-country basis. We will, at the same time, strive for consistency and evenhandedness. We do not have in mind separate sets of criteria for big countries, for weak countries, or for Communist countries.[48]

Such a vague statement of objectives, not surprisingly, led the early Carter initiatives into serious problems. Robert Morris, a member of Henry Kissinger's NSC staff says that the excessively public diplomacy of the first months of the Carter administration caused so much ill will abroad and within the bureaucracy that on April 12, 1977 both Cyrus Vance and Zbigniew Brzezinski met with the President to warn him of the deleterious effects of his policy.[49] Not until late April, presumably as a result of this discussion, was order established so that a less ambiguous formulation and implementation of the human rights policy could begin.

THE CARTER ADMINISTRATION'S VIEW OF HUMAN RIGHTS

The emphasis placed on any special issue in a new administration is the result of the new president's personal style and interests. In this respect the Carter administration was no different from any other. Its standard for a new foreign policy was human rights and very early on the President enunciated five principles which would serve as the policy's guidelines. First, the President argued that the United States had both a legal right and a responsibility under the United Nations Charter and international law to speak out against human rights violations.[50] Second, he rejected the notion of "linkage" as put forth by Kissinger, and averred that the U.S. would pursue human rights objectives simultaneously and independently of its other foreign policy goals.[51] Third, even if the U.S. position strains bilateral relations, the President vowed not to back down. "If we stand for something we ought to be forceful about it. We might win some and lose some in relationships with other countries."[52] Fourth, the President rejected the notion that an increased emphasis on human rights would lead to increased repression.[53] Fifth, Carter argued that an American policy based on fundamental American values would best serve American security interests. Recovering America's lost moral stature was a constant theme of his campaign and of his administration.[54]

These objectives are largely consistent with the mainstream of postwar American foreign policy. The key difference between Carter and his immediate predecessors is not that they had different goals, but that they had different notions of how to achieve them. Whereas Kissinger saw stability as his primary objective—once that had been achieved, then, the possibilities emerged for the pursuit of human rights—for Carter, human rights was the key component of

15

international stability. Kissinger would argue that the promotion of human rights usually did not increase international stability. For Carter, respect for human rights almost by definition improved long-term stability.

Hence, what made the Carter administration unique was not its espousal of a new policy, a common enough tactic used to distinguish current administrations from their predecessors, but the President's firm personal conviction that, as he reported to fellow Southern Baptists in 1978, "I have never detected or experienced any conflict between God's will and my political duty."[5] Convinced that the personal moral sphere was inseparable from the political sphere, the President affirmed that American leadership "need not depend on our inherent military force, or economic power or political persuasion, it should derive from the fact we try to be right and honest and truthful and decent."[56] Not only did the President hold these truths to be self-evident, but he surrounded himself with advisers, particularly in the human rights area, who were convinced of the same. The result was to introduce a very different view of international relations from that conventionally held within the State Department. For sake of continuity, however, human rights could not be proclaimed a totally new policy. Rather, it was said, it had been, to the detriment of the nation, ignored in the recent past, hence the need to reestablish it alongside other traditional American values. Charles W. Maynes, Assistant Secretary of State for International Organization Affairs, claimed that embracing human rights was "not embarking on uncharted ground . . . [but] simply asking that the United States return to that period of forward, balanced, and determined leadership in the field of human rights that we associate with Eleanor Roosevelt."[57] Carter's own belief in the genuine appeal of human rights may have been further bolstered by his belief that it was a typically American sentiment:

> In most ways, there is no such thing as a 'typical American.' In ancestry, religion, color, accent, cultural background—even country of birth—we are as varied as humanity itself. But if any one thing does unite us, it is a common belief in certain human rights.[58]

The new administration quickly sought to bridge the gap between the domestic sphere and the international arena by appointing several noted civil rights activists to key positions in the new human rights machinery emerging in the Department of State. Patricia Derian, head of the new Bureau of Human Rights and Humanitarian Affairs, found a remarkable overlap between what she had experienced as a civil-rights activist in Mississippi and what she found abroad in nations like Argentina.[59] These domestic civil rights activists were chosen because it was felt their prior experiences would be useful to them in their new job. Moreover, many of them shared two common assumptions with international human rights activists: first, that people were essentially the same everywhere and there were no insurmountable obstacles to achieving understanding between them; second, a great optimism in the ability to reform institutions, and through them people, in short order. Abraham Sirkin, a senior human rights official under Carter, quite seriously cites the enthusiasm of a young foreign service officer who during the early days of the Carter administration said, "All that needs to be done is to cable U.S. Embassies around the world: 'The U.S. Government now stands for human rights. Now go ahead and do it.' "[60]

In seeking support for the new human rights policy, much was made of our international obligations under the U.N. Charter, and of the "universal" recognition granted human rights. Congressman Tom Harkin, the author of the human rights restrictions on foreign aid appropriations, argued that through the U.N. Charter, the Universal Declaration of Human Rights and the subsequent human rights covenants and treaties (the Congressman is referring to the International Covenant on Economic, Social and Cultural Rights, and the International Covenant on Civil and Political Rights which have not been ratified by the U.S.),

> Human rights has established a foothold in international affairs. Today, finally I believe it can be said that the rights of individual persons are the primary focus of international law and procedure.[61]

> . . . [T]hese rights are not local U.S. customs; they are all internationally recognized. Every country with which we have relations has approved at least these rights in various international documents. In fact, violation of these rights as a matter of policy is as abhorrent to the world community today as slavery.[62]

Although Harkin is in error about the weight of private individuals in international law, the Carter administration increasingly came to rely on the international legal framework to support its human rights policies. It fit the objectives of Carter's foreign policy well in many respects. The international forum also clearly reflected the interests of the Lesser Developed Nations which the new President was eager to court. Stressing our "obligations" under the U.N. Charter was also a convenient argument to bolster the domestic case for human rights.[63]

At the same time, influential policymakers at home began equating the effectiveness of international public opinion with that of American public opinion. Henry Jackson claimed that:

> Aroused opinion has a power which can sometimes be decisive. We know that the aggregate of official and unofficial efforts can often produce a lever strong enough to move tyrants, to obtain release of prisoners, to reduce harsh sentences, to secure amnesties, and to help those who have vainly sought to emigrate to succeed.[64]

Our ambassador to the United Nations Andrew Young added that, "for perhaps the first time in history we can truly say that there is a worldwide human rights movement and it is steadily gaining force."[65] Although this contradicts the administration's claim that it was embracing a movement that *already* enjoyed world-wide support, the point is that American concern for this issue made it all the more significant.

The administration also argued that human rights violations were important because they reflected an increasingly global problem affecting U.S. national interests.[66] Human rights spokesmen for the administration claimed, for example, that "international terrorism often feeds on human rights grievances within nations."[67] "The fundamental error" which sensitivity to human rights corrects, according to former State Department human rights official Sandra Vogelgesang, is to equate "apparent stability with order and thus to lose sight of long-term U.S. national interest for the sake of short-term advantage."[68] In her judgment, there is a proportionate relationship between intra-state stability and inter-state stability and the price for procrastination may, in fact, be one of the most compelling reasons for stressing attention to human rights. Beginning to deal with violations of human rights can help limit the damage already done by years of disregard for fundamental freedoms and may build the basis for reform that serves long-term U.S. interests.[69] Allard K. Lowenstein, U.S. Ambassador to the U.N. for Special Political Affairs, in summarizing the administration's views on human rights asks, "How can we have peace without human rights?"; and Congressman Harkin echoes this when he decries "... the absurdity of protecting our values by supporting regimes that openly disregard those rights we take to be universal. ..."[70]

Human rights advocates furthermore criticize "realists" like Kennan, Morgenthau, and Niebuhr for neglecting the constructive aspects of morality in their pursuit of the national interests and for their belief that any deliberate effort to act on principle may lead to worse results.[71] *Realpolitik* as practiced by these people is considered "inadequate" and "imprudent."[72] True *Realpolitik*, suggests Vogelgesang, should be broad enough to reflect moral considerations:

> ... human rights falls somewhere between their two perspectives (moral and pragmatic), and between those two perennial poles of alleged contention, power and morality. Promotion of human rights may mean that the two coincide and that the national interest becomes a matter of both pragmatism and principle. Therein lies what may be the most important reason for making human rights a factor of major concern in American diplomacy. It is important because it is *right* in the fullest selfish and selfless sense of that word.[73]

For Vogelgesang, therefore, Kissinger's disregard for human rights contradicted other goals of the Nixon and Ford administrations, such as the search for international stability and avoiding polarization between rich and poor nations, since American support for oppressive regimes offended the very public that Kissinger sought to co-opt into long term support of our policies.[74] On the other hand, advocacy of human rights, she claims, "both serves U.S. national interests" and "spurs needed re-evaluation of that concept."[75]

There is an obvious truth in the assertion that human rights violations reflect the instability of certain regimes. It is much less believable, though, to assert, as some human rights activists do, that a *major* portion of international conflict derives from the derogation of human rights. Conversely, then, it could be said that if human rights were universally respected there would be no further resort to social upheaval, implying an almost millenarian faith in in the importance of human rights. Perhaps, if human rights were defined broadly enough, this would be true, but as it is currently defined in international custom there are many alternative sources of conflict.

By viewing human rights, explicitly or implicitly, not as a policy, but as a condition to be aspired, to human rights activists avoided comparing it with other policies and even with other national objectives. It became exalted, in their minds, by comparison with the routine necessities of everyday conduct of foreign affairs. Patricia Derian, while she was still the State Department's coordinator for human rights, was once quoted as objecting to Secretary of State Vance's suggestion that human rights policies must be guided by the genuine security interests of the United States.[76] For Roberta Cohen, later Deputy Assistant Secretary of State for Human Rights:

> Policies designed solely to protect bases or investments in nations with repressive regimes will have to undergo radical change. In short, if initiatives on behalf of human rights abruptly end where national security considerations begin, the United States will run the risk of discrediting its own policy and of inflicting damage on the entire human rights movement.[77]

Likewise, in response to a question concerning the use of economic assistance to improve human rights conditions, Stephan Oxman, U.S. Executive Assistant to the Deputy Secretary of State twice pointed out that "human rights considerations are not distinct from 'economic' considerations and are more fundamental than mere 'political' consideration" for the Carter administration.[78]

Some congressmen held similar views. In his book *Renewed Concern,* Congressman Paul E. Tsongas urged the United States to discard all its "historic criteria" for aid—stability, political leanings, and strategic interests—and instead to "put respect for human rights at the top of the agenda, and do so openly, publicly, and resolutely."[79] For Congressman Donald Fraser, the policies which ensue as a result of placing the national interest first (as in the case of Chile) are not desirable because they are not based on internal support. In such cases the United States winds up paying double—once for the loss of respect abroad, a second time for disillusionment at home.[80]

It is not surprising, therefore, to find that when converted to practical diplomatic initiatives, Carter human rights concerns touched primarily Third World countries where America's strategic interests were perceived as being slight and its human rights leverage as being greatest. The rhetoric could not be limited to certain countries though, inevitably the administration was asked to justify its human rights policies *vis-à-vis* the Soviet Union and how they affected our security relationship with that country. Although at Notre Dame, the President had declared us "free of that inordinate fear of Communism which once led us to embrace any dictator who joined us in that fear,"[81] for many it was not clear that pointing out

Soviet human rights violations was a better alternative. The administration, though, at least officially, vigorously denied that human rights threatened détente. Jessica Tuchman, a National Security Council staffer at the time, argued that the initial Soviet response was merely an attempt "to scare us into dropping a policy they found uncomfortable. When they saw the President didn't appear likely to do this . . . their protest went way down."[82]

While many critics claimed that stressing human rights would sabotage arms control agreement, Sandra Vogelgesang, for one, contended that U.S.-Soviet arms control agreements should be openly linked to human rights. She argued that since these arguments depend on effective provisions for onsite inspection, "more sustained progress on arms control may not occur until the Soviet system opens up and allows unfettered travel. Next steps in the Strategic Arms Limitations Talks may thus be integrally related to greater protection of human rights."[83] Vogelgesang's proposals demonstrated a greater internal consistency than the eventual Carter policy, which excluded the Soviet Union from the same type of human rights criticism other nations received on the grounds that such criticism might jeopardize arms talks. When Nobel Peace Prize Winner Andrei Sakharov wrote a second letter to President Carter just a few months after their much publicized January correspondence the President did not respond.

Another argument made by at least one administration official in defense of the human rights policy was to speculate what an alternative policy would bring. According to his scenario, without a human rights policy the U.S. government would lose domestic support since "respect for human rights is deeply ingrained in the American psyche." Furthermore, the United State would alienate many around the world "especially idealistic young people" and "future leaders in many countries"; our continued support for oppressive regimes would make enemies of moderate opposition forces which might someday accede to power; and lastly, the "failure of the U.S. government to use its prestige and influence to hold the line against the spread of authoritarianism in the world could facilitate the advent of a political climate that would be adverse to U.S. interests and to the survival of freedom on the entire planet."[84]

Mr. Sirkin, the official in question, overstates his case by attributing to the human rights policy more than it can legitimately take credit for. We might well ask ourselves whether domestic support for our foreign policy is truly founded on human rights; whether human rights has proved to be such an attraction in the Third World; whether it is more important to conduct our policies for today or for those whom it might bring to power tomorrow; and whether the U.S. can truly contain the spread of authoritarian regimes by emphasizing human rights. In each case, current realities argue more against Sirkin than in favor of human rights.

HUMAN RIGHTS AND
FOREIGN ASSISTANCE

The debate over the appropriateness of human rights as a foreign policy objective often overshadowed the problems dawning in another critical area—policy implementation. In determining our new operative policy the administration took into account the likely consequences, the degree of U.S. leverage over the country, our relationship to that regime, the specific cultural and historical conditions of that country, and other U.S. interests.[85] Expectations about human rights performance consequently differed widely from country to country. As a result, the Carter administration preferred to work out its policy through the practice of resolving individual cases rather than by issuing a set of detailed guidelines. In this way, a body of experience comparable to case law gradually becqme the basis for policy decisions. Aside from a policy review memorandum issued early in the summer of 1977, and a presidential Directive of February 1978 providing policy guidelines on the relative merits of different types of aid cutbacks, no broad issues were ever officially addressed, with the result that the so-called "Christopher Group" *de facto* became the highest policy and decision making body for human rights policy.[86]

In evaluating human rights violations the new Bureau of Human Rights and Humanitarian Affairs (HA) was from the outset most visibly associated with pressuring non-Communist countries. This was only natural, since these countries had been the primary focus of the long series of hearings conducted by the Fraser Subcommittee and information about conditions in these areas was more readily available. Congress also found that it could exert greater leverage on those countries dependent on U.S. aid. Human rights groups within the State Department and elsewhere likewise saw that they could exercise the easiest, most definitive, and most visible policy decisions through the foreign aid process. Lastly, the administration's pursuit of détente with the Soviet Union had re-directed most human rights criticisms of the Communist bloc countries into diplomatic channels.[87] As a result, the primary area for implementing the human rights policy became our bilateral and multilateral assistance programs.

The foreign assistance budget came to play a key role in defining the objectives of the human rights policy. The administration tried to develop "specific tactics and objectives for each aid recipient country and revised its procedure for preparing the foreign aid budget to include human rights consideration at the outset along with other U.S. goals and objectives."[88]

Foreign assistance programs generally require legislative authorization and appropriation, and it is the responsibility of the Secretary of State, ultimately, to determine the amount to be requested from the Congress for each nation requesting aid. Each September, therefore, the concerned agencies and bureaus, including the Department of Defense, submit recommendations for the fiscal year to begin in thirteen months.[89] The budget process for economic and security assistance requests begins much as it would in other agencies, with the field officers, who in this case examine human rights conditions in their respective countries. Their evaluations are then sent, along with the embassy's report, to the appropriate State Department Bureau, which processes the request, and, after its own internal human rights review, forwards it to the Christopher Group. Each year, around July, the Group begins its own budget meetings on each country requesting aid. HA staff members sit in on these meetings at both the country and the bureau level as decisions are made on how much aid to request for each country. A working group under the Christopher Group, comprising all concerned representatives and agencies, then screens "virtually every upcoming item of foreign assistance, both bilateral and multilateral." If an unresolved human rights objection is raised the matter is put before the full Interagency Group for a decision. If, after discussion with the Deputy Secretary Christopher, a consensus is not reached the matter is referred to the secretary of state who may decide the matter himself or discuss it with the President.[90] If, as in the majority of cases, there are no objections, the Christopher Group forwards the request for the AID administrator, who then submits this request to the Office of

Management and Budget, which eventually includes it, after consultation with the President, in the annual budget submitted to the Congress.[91] As the human rights legislation has expanded, it has come to include not only foreign assistance, but technology transfer allowances, the granting of Most Favored Nation status, non-tariff concessions, and the extension of duty free import privileges under the U.S. Generalized System of References.[92]

Security assistance programs, by contrast, are reviewed jointly by the Departments of State and Defense. Such requests often originate in DOD, although it is the Secretary of State who decides which countries may enter into such agreements with the United States. Security Assistance programs include: the Military Assistance Program (MAP), the Economic Support Program (ESP), the International Military Education and Training Program (IMET), Foreign Military Sales (FMS), Peacekeeping Operations, and commercial arms sales.[93] At the Defense Department, the Office of International Security Affairs (ISA) takes human rights into account stressing, according to one spokesman, such basic rights as "freedom of person," as well as the deterrence of war.[94] When all proposals have been received by the State Department's Bureau of Politico-Military Affairs, it circulates them among the other bureaus and integrates them into a preliminary budget statement, listing each country's priority for MAP, ESP, IMET, and FMS credits. Peacekeeping funds are kept separately. The combined security assistance package is then distributed to the Arms Export Control Board (AECB) working group, which includes a representative of HA. Here a myriad of factors affecting security decisions are reviewed: foreign policy considerations, national security considerations, the state of the economy, arms control, and human rights concerns. The full AECB then approves the budget which, upon approval by the secretaries of state and defense, goes to the Office of Management and Budget to be included in the annual budget submitted to Congress.[95]

The interdepartmental AECB serves an analogous role to that of the Christopher Group. It was established in 1977 to review all aspects of arms transfer policy and ensure that security assistance conforms with the directives of the president. Permanent members include the Assistant Secretary for Human Rights and representatives from the Bureau of Politico-Military Affairs, the Department of Defense, the NSC, the OMB, Treasury, the CIA and the Arms Control and Disarmament Agency. The AECB is charged with policy planning as well as review functions. If, as occasionally occurs, the

AECB did not reach a consensus, the request is referred to the Christopher Group.[96]

The more controversial FMS requests are usually approved in close collaboration with the State Department. As far as human rights are concerned, each time the proposal passes through the AECB, it is reviewed by the HA representative there. In addition, according to a study by the Congressional Research Service, "it is common practice for other participants from regional bureaus, DOD, etc., to include human rights considerations in their analysis of U.S. interests in connection with the proposed sale."[97]

REORGANIZING THE STATE DEPARTMENT

Although the skeleton of human rights machinery had already been created by Congress in the form of a Deputy Director for Human Rights Affairs, an officer assigned to the International Organizations Bureau, an Interagency Group on Human Rights and Foreign Assistance[98] and human rights officers attached to bureaus, the new administration quickly expanded the human rights machinery on its own initiative. To ensure a direct link with the President, a full-time NSC staff member was to serve as a liaison between the White House and the State Department on human rights issues.[99] Furthermore, Secretary Vance directed the department's Policy Planning Staff to formulate a "broad human rights policy" whose concepts, Senator Daniel Patrick Moynihan acidly commented, were to become "as integral to American foreign policy as is Marxism-Leninism to Soviet... operations and planning."[100] Among the issues the Planning Staff was to examine were: the definition of human rights, attempting to combine U.S. notions of human rights as primarily civil and political rights with Third World concepts; ways to promote economic rights; how to balance different human rights priorities and examining various modes of influence; the interrelationship of human rights and national security issues; the global application of human rights; and lastly, monitoring international compliance with human rights standards.

In February 1977, Secretary Vance requested that all bureaus compile strategy papers on "key human rights problems in their areas and tactics for dealing with them."[101] A year later, after many false starts, the President, under the prodding of Assistant Secretary Patricia Derian, issued a secret directive ordering all government agencies to consider the impact of their decisions on human rights abroad.[102]

The most significant management innovations, however, came not in the plethora of new directives, but in the creation of a permanent body of human rights monitors within the State Department: the Bureau of Human Rights and Humanitarian Affairs (HA). The head of the new bureau, former civil rights activist Patricia Derian, promptly received the title of Assistant Secretary of State. The Bureau had three sub-divisions: an Office of Human Rights, an Office of Refugee and Migration Affairs, and a section responsible for POWs/MIAs. The initial staff amounted to over thirty people, approximately ten of whom dealt exclusively with human rights issues.[103] Each sub-division was headed by a Deputy Assistant Secretary of State. In 1978, a fourth branch and a new Deputy Assistant Secretary for Human Rights and Security Assistance were added.[104]

Derian and the HA spearheaded the drive to institutionalize human rights in foreign policy decisionmaking. She was known to have direct access to the President, a fact which lent greater weight to her recommendations. Human rights concerns quickly became a part of most strategy papers and policy statements. A directive was sent to all ambassadors assigning them personal responsibility for following up on the requirements of the human rights policy.[105] Outside HA, human rights officers were assigned to each of the State Department's bureaus and to the Legal Adviser's Office, where they were to call attention to the requirements of the law.[106] A new human rights bureaucracy sprang up not only within State, but also in Commerce, Defense, and other departments.

Virtually all government agencies that dealt with foreign agents soon had some sort of human rights restrictions on their books. Among the most prominent agencies affected by the new legislation were:

The *Agency for International Development,* which is empowered to offer bilateral economic assistance to countries. In making sure that its assistance conforms with human rights requirements, the AID human rights coordinator reviews a country's overall human rights record and trends. The budget review process plays an important role in allocating AID funds. The country-by-country review process endorsed by the Carter administration is cited by AID officials as being much more comprehensive than the project appraisal document; country allocations are also seen as more significant than project allocations. The funds proposed by AID are subsequently reviewed by the Interagency Group for Human Rights and

Humanitarian Affairs three months before final submission to Congress.[107]

The *Overseas Private Investment Corporation,* or OPIC, which was created by the Foreign Assistance Act of 1969 and formally recognized as an independent agency two years later, was formed to assist U.S. private investors in making investments in Third World countries by ensuring them against risk.[108] Since 1978 all OPIC projects have been screened for human rights considerations by its Insurance or Finance Departments, then by the Development Office, and lastly by HA, which, it if has any objections, refers the matter to the Interagency Group.[109]

The *Export-Import Bank.* Ex-Im Bank programs are designed to supplement government exports when the private sector is incapable of providing sufficient funds for a foreign customer's needs. As of 1979, only Uruguay, Chile, and Argentina were automatically denied Ex-Im Bank loans on human rights grounds.[110]

Other international financial institutions (IFIs) subject to human rights scrutiny are: the International Bank for Reconstruction and Development Association (the World Bank, or IBRD), the International Development Association (IDA), the International Financial Corporation (IFC), and the three regional banks—the Inter-American Development Bank (IDB), the African Development Fund (ADF) and the Asian Development Bank (ADB).

The second important institutional addition to the State Department under the Carter aministration was the Interagency Group on Human Rights and Humanitarian Affairs ("Christopher Group"), named after its head, Deputy Secretary of State Warren Christopher. It was established by a National Security Council Directive of April 1, 1977 to examine U.S. bilateral and multilateral foreign assistance programs in the light of human rights conditions, provide guidance with respect to specific decisions on assistance, and in general coordinate the administration's position in this area.[111] It included a member of the NSC staff, persons from Treasury, Defense, Commerce, Agriculture, and Labor, and representatives at the World Bank and the Inter-American Development Bank.[112] The Christopher Group had neither a large structure nor staff. Deputy Secretary Christopher exercised ultimate control, and the Group operated on a case-by-case basis which was very time consuming and often forced officials to deal with trivial appropriations items. Its decisions were usually elaborated by subordinate working groups which met two to four times a month to review bilateral and multilateral projects forwarded from the Treasury Department.[113] All foreign aid requests were reviewed by the Christopher Group, whose basic criterion in approving aid requests was to establish whether the aid will go to the needy. If this claim could be sustained by the sponsoring agency, the project would most likely be approved despite a recipient country's poor human rights record.[114] Likewise, if it was the determination of the Group that the general observance of human rights in that country was improving, it would recommend approval.

The long-term objectives of those active in the human rights policy could be broadly divided into policy modifying objectives and organizational/legislative objectives. The first set of objectives was based on the premise that ignoring oppression in other countries significantly increased the "risk that its successor will be hostile to our interests."[115]

It was the intent of the human rights people to eventually incorporate their principles into the formulation of U.S. foreign policy so that those concerned with human rights could be relieved of "fire-fighting," i.e., having to focus on individual cases—and get on with the "much broader battle for the fostering of more open and competitive political systems."[116] Abraham Sirkin distinguishes between a "maximum human rights agenda—the democratization of all the nations of the world and the fulfillment of the basic needs of their people"[117] and what is achievable in the short run. For many of its promoters, human rights was an issue ideally suited to bridge the gap between actual conditions and the desired state of world affairs because it was a "sustained effort to get at the roots of repression, to stop the flow of political and economic refugees and the regional and international tension and terrorism."[118] Human rights was thus billed at least by some, as a panacea for all current and future world problems.

Skepticism about the new priorities soon abounded both within and outside the government, however. At the first Foreign Service Institute human rights training seminar many participants remained unreceptive to the new policy, calling it "moral imperialism" and "harmful" to more important foreign policy goals. Roberta Cohen concluded that a "sustained reeducation of the department will be needed to overcome deep-rooted resistance to the integration of human rights in foreign policy."[119] Here we encounter the organizational/legislative aspect of the human rights drive: the desire "to encompass the entire Executive Branch including DOD, CIA, Justice, Treasury, with each department and agency . . . required to make available to the State Department its human rights information for inclusion in reports to Congress and for use in overall planning."[120]

A conscious attempt was thus made to restructure the foreign policy apparatus and to reeducate policymakers. Congressman Harkin urged that "our human rights actions must rest on more than the philosophy of one administration. It must become as institutionalized a foreign policy consideration as national security and economic well-being are now."[121] He hoped that Congress would enact a "body of human rights laws that will become the cornerstone of future laws and will guide future policy."[122] Eventually, from being the cornerstone of our laws, these enactments were to become the cornerstone of the United Nations. Despite its lack of enforcement capabilities, in the mind of many human rights spokesmen the United Nations still represented "the best long-term hope for a system of constraints on governments and for protecting human rights."[123]

THE CARTER HUMAN RIGHTS
POLICY IN RETROSPECT

Many who disagree with the former President's emphasis on human rights judge the results as either inadequate or contradictory. Others contend that it caused organizational chaos in our foreign policy apparatus. These two types of criticism, however, address the effects of the policy rather than the policy itself. Defenders of the policy claim in their defense that under different circumstances or given more time, the human rights policy could blossom to its full potential. The problems resulting from the pursuit of four years of human rights policy under the previous administration, however, have a more deep-rooted flaw in their perception of international reality. Since this criticism is potentially more damaging than those formulated on the basis of the results of the policy, it is worth examining in some detail.

Some argue that human rights as pursued by the Carter administration go against American legal and political traditions. The notion that individuals have political rights as such, apart from the state or the church, is a relatively modern idea.[124] Until the Middle Ages it was common knowledge that there was a moral law, above the laws of the State, by which the ruler was judged. By contrast, the contemporary notion that rights belong to every citizen of the state (more recently amended to presume rights for every person regardless of citizenry) is essentially secular in origin. It reflects a common post-Enlightenment refusal to accept a permanent separation of the morally ideal from the politically actual.[125]

Although human rights are a concept of contemporary Western culture, this is not to say, as Charles Frankel pointed out, that they are parochial.[126] It would certainly be an overstatement to say that these ideas emerged nowhere but in the West. But it is not an overstatement to say that only in the West have these ideas acquired a dominant position in law, constitution-making and ideological debate.[127] The objectivity of human rights as a universal standard for action is further complicated by the view, traditionally held by Americans, that human rights are those enumerated in the Bill of Rights.[128] Indeed, the United States has traditionally opposed the incorporation of economic rights widely accepted by other countries, into the concept of human rights. In giving socio-economic rights prominence, and by accepting the notion that such rights exist even though a court of law might not be able to provide a remedy for violations, the Carter administration contravened a long-standing Anglo-Saxon legal tradition.[129] Perhaps even more fundamental is the incompatibility that seems to exist between political freedom, publicly linked by the Congress and the administration to *laissez* faire economics, and the international call for socio-economic justice and redistribution of the world's wealth. America's deeply rooted policies of free trade and a powerful private sector, David Forsythe argues, can never be as popular world-wide as Carter expected them to be.[130]

Few would question a nation's rights to comment publicly on human rights conditions in other countries and most international jurists would agree that by signing the United Nations Charter and other agreements nations accept certain obligations. There is much less international support, though, for the Carter administration's interpretation that these treaties *compel* nations to monitor each other's human rights behavior. Reviewing this nation's diplomatic practice of the past two centuries, Norman Graebner writes that, "Perhaps it was true, as Vance once suggested, that the message of the American Revolution had encouraged and inspired other nations and peoples.[131] That, however, had never been a matter of foreign policy."[132]

President Carter and his key aides in the State Department were so thoroughly convinced of the rightness and appropriateness of human rights that justifications were superfluous to them. It soon became clear that the human rights policy had become an objective unto itself. Advocates of the policy dwelt less on the actual state of the world than on the possible future if human rights were neglected, without asking themselves how we can mold future realities while overlooking present ones. Deputy Secretary of State Warren Christopher, the chief implementer of the human rights policy in the State Department, defended the administration's view on this:

Shambaugh Library

Our strength as a Nation and our magnetism to the world at large are predicated on our commitment to human rights ... the pursuit of this cause is not an ideological luxury cruise with no practical port of call. Our idealism and self-interest coincide. Widening the circle of countries which share our human rights values is at the very core of our security interests. Such nations make strong allies. Their commitment to human rights gives them an inner strength and stability which causes them to stand steadfastly with us on the most difficult issues of our time.[133]

Although this may be an adequate domestic justification for our policy, human rights proponents did not always fully consider whether our pursuit of humanitarian policies would be perceived as such by other nations. The persistent assumption by the Carter administration that peace and human rights were in a symbiotic relationship is unfortunately belied by international society, which finds enough sources of conflict to dwell upon apart from human rights issues. The major lesson which the Carter administration claims to have learned from Vietnam—the deleterious effects of a policy pursued for its own sake rather than for specific American objectives—seems to have been lost in Carter's implementation of the human rights policy.

One often gets the sense that in their attempts to implement human rights under Carter, policymakers viewed the "traditional" conduct of foreign affairs as their major obstacle. In their determined efforts to instill the notion that human rights was a distinct and vital area of consideration, human rights officials openly debunked such concepts as "national security," and "economic interests." Not surprisingly, therefore, human rights initiatives often met with strong opposition in the State Department. Whereas other programs were seen by State Department officials as aimed at advancing identifiable political, economic, or security interests of the United States, the human rights policy was seen as designed to further exclusively its own goals while making the work of others more difficult.[134] Characteristic of this attitude was Ambassador Malcolm Toon's reply to reporters when asked why he did not invite Nobel laureate Andrei Sakharov to the American Embassy reception in Moscow on July fourth: "My job is to get along with the Soviet government."[135]

Conflicting attitudes over the role human rights should play in our relations with the Soviet Union surfaced early on in the administration. Marshall Shulman, the State Department's chief Soviet Affairs specialist, and Zbigniew Brzezinski, National Security

Adviser to the President, were both said to view human rights as posing unacceptable strains on Soviet society.[136] Syndicated columnist Patrick Buchanan succinctly captured the tensions within our policy when he wrote:

> The Carter administration doesn't seem to appreciate that when the President hails political dissent, he is indeed waging ideological war on the Soviet Union. . . . For Carter to encourage and cheer on competing centers of political thought is to strike at the legitimacy of the Soviet state. . . . they can no more tolerate competing opposition centers of political power inside Russia than can the Roman Catholic Church tolerate a second, or third, or fourth pope.[137]

A similar assessment of Carter's policies led the British International Institute for Strategic Studies to comment worriedly that "If Mr. Carter's campaign were to confront the Soviet Union with the choice of either continuing détente abroad or maintaining domestic and bloc control at home, the priority would be unquestioned."[138]

The inconsistencies that eventually developed in the Carter administration's human rights practices reflected the realities of strategic geopolitics more than administration spokesmen care to admit. Norman Graebner has noted that "if a generalized response to human rights violations exceeded the possibilities of policy formulation, a selective response invited charges of hypocrisy."[139] The pattern of American conduct that resulted was conditioned not only by security considerations, but also by the bureaucratic struggle among the various groups clamoring for an input into policymaking. Though such struggles are not unusual, a Congressional Research Staff report concluded that "their scope and intensity seem to have been especially great in the human rights arena because of the unconventional character and the vagueness of applicable policy guidelines."[140] Though some administration apologists have argued lamely that the Carter administration pursued a policy of "deliberate inconsistencies,"[141] others acknowledged bluntly that, indeed, countries like Nicaragua remained the target of American pressure because U.S. cars do not run on bananas.[142]

The view of human rights as both an ideal and as a policy led to much confusion among even staunch supporters of the concept. Niels C. Nielsen, Jr., Chairman of the Religious Studies Department at Rice University, has made a distinction between ideals and rights:

"An ideal is something one can aim at, but cannot by definition immediately realize. A right, on the contrary, is something that can, and from the moral point of view, must be respected here and now."[143] It is important to bear in mind this distinction between what is a desirable "good" and what is a "right." Not every "good" is a "right," nor is it wise to strive to make goods rights. Rights impose the obligation of fulfillment, and too many rights would present conflicting obligations, which if strictly enforced, would make life unbearable.[144]

The fact that rights presume an obligation is no less true for human rights,[145] a fact which poses a tremendous strain on policymakers and partly explains the inversion of traditional foreign policy priorities among some human rights activists. As an ideal, human rights inevitably conflicts with other obligations of policymakers, who must view it as one moral standard alongside other moral standards (e.g., the prevention of nuclear war, the preservation of peace and stability in the world, diminishing world hunger and poverty, etc.) by which to conduct our policy.

Some human rights advocates have, as a result of the Carter experience, reduced their expectations for a human rights policy. J. Bryan Hehir, Associate Secretary for International Justice and Peace, U.S. Catholic Conference, has proposed only two sets of guidelines for our human rights policy. First, that human rights not be envisioned as a means of projecting U.S. values (i.e., pluralistic democracy) abroad, but, rather, as a standard of restraint limiting our cooperation with repressive regimes. Second, that human rights objectives be systematically weighed against other considerations.[146] Former Congressman Donald Fraser has suggested that a renewed human rights policy should be judged on the basis of its results, rather than by moral commitment.[147] For Douglas Maclean the moral criteria for a human rights policy are not that crucial, for human rights can be defended even from a non-moral perspective:

> We need only to recognize that there are some positive duties, that somebody ought to come to the aid of the victims of oppressive governments. There is no question about evaluating types of governments and imposing the types we happen to like on the other nations or cultures, not unless torturing and detaining political dissidents without trial are essential to some types of government that a culture supports.[148]

Having identified a crucial issue, Maclean refuses to discuss further why governments persist in violating human rights. Former human rights official Sandy Vogelgesang, however, offers this very perceptive observation:

> To put it bluntly, governments violate human rights because their leaders believe it is in their interests to do so. Dictators need not be diabolical devotees of torture to conclude that it is often cheaper or easier to jail opponents or terrorize citizenry, rather than meet popular demands.[149]

This is the predicament which the human rights policymakers under Carter could not resolve. On a philosophical level their faith in human progress led them to reject the view that there might be insurmountable differences between cultures that precluded universal acceptance of human rights. Yet, on a practical level this precept set an impossible task before the policy: to mitigate the fears of all repressive leaders around the world so that they would eventually find respect for human rights more attractive than repression. It is difficult to even imagine what sort of incentives might be offered to the various world rulers to induce them to change their internal policies. Whatever they might be, they were certainly beyond the capabilities of even the United States.

In terms of management objectives, what should have been a veritable bureaucratic revolution greatly increased tensions within the State Department, but otherwise had surprisingly little practical effect. Having pledged during his campaign to double foreign assistance programs his first year and increase them by 50% over the next several years, President Carter managed to increase his foreign assistance budget by only 15% his first year.[150] Yet, despite this setback, his administration persisted in strengthening and expanding legislation. Some examples: Section 701 of the International Financial Institutions Act of 1977 requires U.S. executive directors at IFIs to vote against assistance to any government that violates basic human rights. Since, then, the United States has opposed over thirty loans to countries through IFIs, and half a dozen other loans have been withdrawn from consideration.[151] In 1978, aid was withheld from Vietnam, Uganda, Cambodia, Cuba, Laos, Angola, Brazil and Argentina, and was reduced for Uruguay, El Salvador, Guatemala, and the Philippines as a result of the requirements of the Foreign Assistance Act.[152]

Despite the increased burden that human rights considerations placed on foreign policy decisionmaking, and the strain it put on our relations with certain countries, President Carter held fast to his position that the policy was good for the country. There was something dynamic and electrifying about refusing to accept the status quo and being seized by an idea which, "placed the United States once again at the center of a movement which for two generations—it can be said for a century or more—has animated men and women of good will, obscure and eminent, from many different lands."[153]

The Carter administration also claimed significant improvements in human rights conditions around the world as a result of its concern for human rights. According to spokesmen, "heartening reports were forthcoming from a number of countries indicating that repressive practices had been eased in response to the U.S. campaign; significant numbers of political prisoners were reported to have been released and long overdue judicial reforms enacted."[154] National Security Adviser Zbigniew Brzezinski cited "tangible progress in at least 40 countries around the world in which 2½ billion people live."[155] In his report to Congress in January 1978, Secretary Vance cited results which he felt could be attributed directly to the human rights policy: a more intense focus on human rights by world leaders; the emergence of human rights as a major theme of discussion at international organizations and conferences; the inclusion of human rights as a subject of national debate in many countries, as well as the easing of repression, release of prisoners, and increased liberalization of many authoritarian regimes. President Carter summarized the overall benefits of the policy when he said:

> The human rights policy is the flagship of the Administration's foreign policy, popular among the American public; attracting support from significant sectors in many developing countries; strengthening the U.S. image in the world. It is a strong link between our ideals and our self-interest.[156]

For critics, however, the damage far outweighed the benefits. A focal point of such criticism was the State Department itself. Three factors exacerbated institutional tensions within the Department. Firstly, human rights injected yet another competing interest in an already complicated process; one, moreover, which went against traditional diplomatic notions and greatly increased problems for other bureaus. Secondly, other functional institutions, (AID, Treasury, the IFIs) had their own programs which HA had been designed to either suppress or re-direct toward its own needs. Thirdly, many officials within the Department decried the lack of a coherent policy statement.[157] Bureau officials criticized HA officials for being blind to other foreign policy considerations; conversely, the HA suspected regional officials of clientelism and wanting to maintain cordial relations at the expense of broader American interests.

Another institutional complaint often raised by State Department and other officials was the wasteful redundancy in human rights reporting. Annual reports were to be supplied by the Departments of State and Treasury, by OPIC, by the IMF supplementary facility and other international financial institutions. A CRS study found that reporting requirements were continually expanded so that the numerous annual reports were supplemented by one-time requests: e.g., when the U.S. enters into consultations on aid agreements with foreign countries; on the staffing and operations of HA; on the proposals for reforming and expanding UN human rights activities; on the harassment of U.S. journalists abroad; on U.S. policies toward the Soviet Union.[158] In each case, the result is several weeks delay in processing aid requests.

Thirdly, the human rights policy impinged upon the State Department's internal morale. Tension was heightened by the fact that none of the new human rights appointees were senior level officials who could lend authority and experience to the new policy. For many this was their first experience with international relations. On the other hand, State Department personnel had not been adequately prepared; they lacked both training in and commitment to the new policy.[159] Career foreign service officers pointed out the strained situation that arose in bureaus and embassies when an agency charged with maintaining good relations with a country also had to prepare reports for public release on human rights violations in that country.[160]

The CRS study concludes that the administration's heavy emphasis on human rights led to "factionalism and many bitter debates within the Councils of Government, especially during the first year of the Carter Administration."[161] Relations between the HA and the Bureau of East Asian and Pacific Affairs, and the Bureau of Inter-American Affairs remained difficult throughout the Carter administration.[162]

The use of aid requests to influence human rights behavior was frequently criticized as being too inflexible. The average length of the Department of Defense's security assistance planning cycle is 28 months, with several years required to negotiate contracts, produce and export the equipment. In one particular instance, when Public Law 95-88 inaugurated human rights requirements for Title I food aid shipments under PL 480, the Department of State began to review the records of 28 countries scheduled to receive such shipments in 1978. The result was several weeks delay in the signing of bilateral agreements and much frustration abroad, in the Departments of State and Agriculture, and among congressional representatives from the farming states, who were concerned lest farm exports drop.[163]

Some of the damage to U.S. programs cited by regional officers included loss of interest in export markets among U.S. businessmen, increased paperwork and the questioning of U.S. reliability among foreign purchasers.[164] Joseph Karth has estimated losses to U.S. industry as a result only of aborted military sales as having reached $800 million by 1979.[165] Although some improvements might be possible, a congressional research study concluded that, "much of the tension . . . seems to be inherent in the use of aid for human rights ends."[166]

Although some countries improved their observance of human rights under American pressure, others felt persecuted by the new policy. In 1977 Brazil, El Salvador, Guatemala, Argentina and Uruguay decided they would no longer accept any U.S. assistance on the grounds that their citation in the State Department's country reports insulted their national dignity. Guatemala eventually reversed its decision and U.S. aid to that country was quickly restored with no apparent reappraisal of human rights conditions there.[167] Even in those countries where conditions did improve, Congressman Fraser noted that these were usually surface improvements that left the institutional arbitrariness of the regime untouched.[168] If, as occasionally happened, it became known that a government had bowed to external pressure over human rights, that government became intransigent in future negotiations.

Congress nevertheless passed a considerable amount of human rights legislation prohibiting sales to particular countries. Much to its dismay, however, it often found its intent frustrated by the fact that aid appropriations are not fully under its control. Of a total $1.6 billion allocated to South Korea in 1976, only $347 million, or 22% was directly authorized by Congress. Out of a total of $72 billion received by ten major aid recipients, only $868 million (12%) was provided by direct congressional action. The rest came from eight semi-autonomous, self-sustaining U.S. government corporations and agencies.[169] International bank loans were often used to counteract the effects of Congressional aid cuts, as in the case of Argentina, where aid was reduced by $17 million, yet the Argentine government proceeded to get $235 million in loans from the World Bank, the Inter-American Development Bank and the IMF. Similarly, when the

United States suspended aid to Chile during the critical years of 1974-76, the World Bank and the IMF provided credits to of almost $366 million.[170]

Most people involved in the process agree that the use of foreign assistance as the *primary* means of fostering human rights abroad is clearly inappropriate. It places too great a burden on the budget which, in this context, is better used as a policy statement than as an instrument of policy. This is a crucial difference between the domestic arena and the international arena. Domestically, budget cuts are often used to direct policy changes. The domestic recipient of aid usually has nowhere to go for funds except the federal government. Internationally, however, there are many countries and lending agencies to which countries can turn for aid. We overestimate our value to countries by linking good behavior on human rights to foreign aid, and many countries let us know it.

Studies have shown that in implementing change, management usually does very little planning on how to overcome resistance to the impending change. The human rights policy under Carter is a classic example of this. In its defense, the Carter administration could point out that the State Department cannot shut down for a period of time to reorganize. Our obligations abroad persist indefinitely. Former President Carter is perhaps most at fault for having exploited the issue of human rights so vociferously during his campaign that he was obliged to implement it or face sharp domestic criticism.

When the President chose to implement it, though, he did so by fiat. He organized a distinct bureaucracy within the State Department and appointed to it people widely perceived within State as ill-suited to diplomacy. Moreover, he gave the newcomers authority over many senior State Department officials. The result—the President's new directives were thwarted from the outset. Despite public statements that the United States would unilaterally reduce arms sales and impose ceilings on military transfers, such sales rose steadily during the Carter administration. Foreign assistance, a major arm of the human rights policy, was only rarely withheld during the compilation of the budget in the departments, on the grounds that stopping aid would damage "national security." Whenever aid was withheld, the country usually got the funds it needed through IFIs, including, paradoxically, semiautonomous U.S. government agencies.

The impression that the policy was incoherent and poorly managed was further fostered by mid-level bureaucrats to justify the pursuit of their traditional objectives. One might conclude from the overall level of foreign assistance allocated during the Carter years that despite presidential and congressional predisposition in favor of human rights, there was little either could do, ultimately, to prevent international financing of another country's programs.

The fact that many prominent human rights activists totally identified the human rights policy with morality only exacerbated the dilemmas facing policymakers. By defining human rights as the objective that legitimized our foreign policy its proponents subordinated all other considerations. It does our sense of morality an injustice, however, to restrict it to the objectives of any one policy. Morality is a much broader concept than human rights. It includes values rooted in the history and culture of each nation. Views on decency, ethics, and individual conduct are all part of morality, and they often differ from culture to culture. Many human rights advocates presume that a general agreement on certain basic human rights implies the existence of a common moral system for all mankind. The human rights covenants and agreements already reached are, for them, the first steps toward a universal code of conduct, both internal and external, for all nations, which would eventually become the basis for a stable and harmonious world order.

Alas, the reality we face today is much bleaker. Differences in culture and tradition appear to be strengthening around the world. They exacerbate, rather than diminish tensions, even between cultures as close as those of Jews and Moslems. Our sense of common morality is still too abstract and too weak to obviate conflict in today's world, and the human rights agreements we have reached seem to be the very limit of the goals statesmen pay lip service to, rather than the earnest foundations for the future.

It is unrealistic to accept human rights agreements as a sufficient guarantee for this or any other nation's security. Toward the end of his term President Carter too came to realize, as all statesmen must, that our obligation to the peace and prosperity of our generation take precedence when they conflict with our strivings for the still distant goal of a just international society. President Carter's great service to human rights was to bring it to the forefront of international politics. Subsequent administrations must now attempt to refine our approach to this objective, and make it consistent with immediate as well as long term American goals.

REDEFINING HUMAN RIGHTS

One of the lasting effects of the Carter presidency has been make human rights an almost unquestioned component of our foreign policy. The debate over human rights as it has continued under Reagan asks not whether this country should have a human rights policy but, given that we shall pursue human rights, how should we maximize the benefits and minimize the damage to our diplomacy?

Two contending voices on human rights matters could be distinguished within in the Carter administration. One was that of Secretary Vance, who urged moderation and recognition of the limits of national power in the pursuit of our ideals. Another was that of influential presidential appointee Patricia Derian, who perceived the foreign policy establishment as ineluctably opposed to human rights and hence saw it as her duty to proclaim human rights in the faces of all those who "don't understand our system and democratic ways," meaning especially the Pentagon, the CIA, and the NSC staff.[171] As Richard Cohen, a senior member of her staff, expressed it:

> If there is a middle ground on the issue [of human rights] it is that you adhere to a human rights policy until you simply cannot—until it leads you either into a foreign policy debacle or into a situation where by trying to impose a policy we lose all leverage.[172]

The obvious inconsistency between the Human Rights Bureau's public statements and the policies of the administration only aggravated Carter's foreign policy problems. When Ronald Reagan was elected in 1980, while he supported human rights which he had endorsed as a candidate in 1976, many of his key advisers felt that a gap had arisen between our proclamations and our possibilities, a gap that limited the effectiveness of the human rights policy by raising unrealistic expectations. Inevitably perhaps, this judgement was seen as an excuse to desert the cause by those who perceived human rights as the pre-eminent goal of American foreign policy. The new President and his advisers, nonetheless, set out to reconstruct the entire human rights policy, beginning with its philosophical assumptions, to bring it into greater accordance with their perception of American values and American security interests.

The administration's new approach was first expounded by Ernest W. Lefever, Reagan's nominee to replace Pat Derian, and soon ran into the opposition of Congress, which felt that the President intended to downgrade human rights. The President sought to reassure Congress that his review of the human rights policy was not engendered by a lessening of concern for human rights violations. At a White House ceremony commemorating the Jewish victims of Nazi death camps, the President departed from his prepared text to say: "Wherever it takes place in the world, the persecution of people, for whatever reason—persecution of people for their religious belief—that is a matter to be on the negotiating table or the United States does not belong at that table."[173] Administration concern was later reiterated in its first human rights status report submitted to Congress in 1982, which stated categorically that "this Administration believes that human rights is an issue of central importance both to relieve suffering and injustice and to link foreign policy with the traditions of the American people."[174]

While nominally human rights continues to be a major concern of this administration, Ronald Reagan has hesitated to embrace the human rights issue as unreservedly as his predecessor. He has often repeated that there are many ways for human rights concerns to manifest themselves and many limitations to what we can expect to accomplish through human rights alone. For example, the Reagan administration argues that we fulfill one human rights obligation by simply being one of the world's rarest phenomena: a successful democracy that respects human rights. Yet, despite our wealth and power, administration spokesmen insist, we must constantly remind ourselves that our resources and influences are limited. It is not within our purview to change radically the way other governments behave. Our sovereignty ends with our own borders. Thus, while striving to improve ourselves and the conditions of others around the world, we should acknowledge that we live in a tragic world and realize that as a country we can only mitigate suffering, not eradicate it.[175] An underlying assumption of the current administration is that even universal respect for human rights will not automatically resolve a host of other foreign and domestic problems that plague humanity. This thought is succinctly captured in Michael Novak's conclusion that human rights do not exist as an ideology.[176] It lies at the heart of a recent administration statement that " 'Human Rights' is today the term with which most of those yearning for justice and for relief from oppression voice their hopes . . . But we must understand that it is a cause with a recent origin and short history."[177]

An effective human rights policy, the Reagan administration insists, must be integrated into our national security policy. Perceptions of American prestige and success, along with our ability to defend our own freedom from outside aggression, directly influence the success of our human rights efforts. Thus, this administration seems to tie measures aimed at promoting our own freedom and security to those promoting human rights, an effort the Carter administration could never credibly make while it was questioning rising defense expenditures.

Like his predecessor, Ronald Reagan seeks to encourage changes in the policies of foreign states, in the belief that obviating the necessity of resorting to human rights violations ultimately enhances human rights. But, as opposed to what at times seemed like a blind faith in the justness of revolutionary change among Carter aides, the Reagan administration argues that pursing reforms too quickly could in some cases result in a worsening rather than an improvement of human rights conditions. Elliott Abrams cites pre-Hitlerite Germany as an example of this: "The founders of the Weimar Republic, by aiming at a democracy stripped of all the authoritarian features of Imperial Germany, created a system so fragile that it was overwhelemed by something wholly barbaric in only fourteen years. . . ."[178]

Thus, a human rights policy, unless it is painstakingly elaborated, runs not only the danger of being ineffective, but also of being counter-productive. Moreover, the dangers to human rights today stem not only from over eager domestic reformers, but, say the Reagan officials, from totalitarian aggression eager to exploit any potentially unstable domestic situations in a manner favorable to itself. One authoritative government publication has suggested that we are today facing a historically unprecedented situation: not only has the pre-World War I consensus on huamn rights been shattered by the emergence of totalitarian regimes among the major powers, but now the leading totalitarian state, the U.S.S.R., has the technical capability to extend its influence to any region of the globe.[179] According to United States Ambassador to the United Nations Jeanne J. Kirkpatrick:

> The result of these parallel developments, in the Soviet Union and the United States, culminating in Ronald Reagan's election as president is *that the return of American self-confidence in the nation's fundamental principles and approach, and the determination to defend these principles in the world, coincide with a period of unprecedented Soviet expansion and power.* They also coincide with dramatic new evidence from Poland concerning the ultimate vulnerability of the Marxist-Leninist one-party state and the vulnerability of the Soviet empire, to precisely those human inclinations to freedom and self-determination that are enshrined in the Western liberal democratic tradition. . . .[180]

This assessment by Ambassador Kirkpatrick highlights a significant difference between the human rights policies of Carter and Reagan. Whereas, for Carter the United States had for too long been "inordinately fearful" of Communism, for the current administration the philosophical and political differences between our two systems have not significantly eroded. The Communist political system remains unworthy of human kind,[181] and the current administration seems intent on reviving the concept of "totalitarian" states, even though the term has fallen into disrepute among political scientists.

A distinctive feature of the twentieth century has been the emergence of the totalitarian state. Prior to 1914, the Reagan administration argues,"there was a perceived legitimacy to the principles [of human rights] that caused each of these countries [including Imperial Russia] to develop in the direction of greater equality before the law and more and more scrupulous adherence to human rights."[182] War shattered the cohesiveness of civilization and brought to power, first in Russia then in Germany, regimes that were not only opposed to but antithetical to the Judaeo-Christian tradition. While Nazi aggression spent itself during the Second World War, the yearned for era of enduring world peace remained a distant goal as Western leaders came to realize that Communist Russia shared few Western assumptions about human nature. "Thus a world in which several major powers were in theoretical agreement over human rights has given way to a world in which the two great powers are fundamentally divided over this issue."[183]

Many states have been called totalitarian since Hannah Arendt and

Carl J. Friedrich first brought the term to public prominence in the 1930's—so many, in fact, that scholars in recent years have come to regard the term as almost meaningless. For the Reagan administration, however, the term retains its distinctiveness, and early in the administration its spokesmen elaborated on the distinction between totalitarian and authoritarian states and how this distinction should affect American foreign policy.

According to Ernest W. Lefever, human rights adviser to the Reagan transition team and unsuccessful nominee to head the State Department's human rights bureau:

> A totalitarian state by definition admits no other center of authority, control, taste, or thought. The only freedom of choice is the narrow range that does not challenge the one central authority. The totalitarian state by definition—that is not my opinion but by dictionary definition—is one that replaces the role of the family, the school, he church, the university, the economy, all power centers, whereas in an authoritarian state there are islands of freedom, there are places of choice. . . .[184]

Responding to an article by Philip Geyelin in *The Washington Post,* William Gavin impugned totalitarian regimes even more sharply:

> Human rights violations in totalitarian regimes are not only atrocities themselves but also a means of strengthening and penetrating the ideologically motivated struggle against the West and its values. Human rights abuse in authoritarian regimes, bestial as they are, does not serve as a means of fostering a philosophy of conquest against the rest of the world. . . . An authoritarian regime must always be condemned for evils it inflicts on its citizens. But a totalitarian regime must be condemned not only for what it *does* but for what it *is.*[185]

The administration argues that totalitarian regimes are far worse than authoritarian regimes since they exercise more complete control over the minds and actions of their subjects by not allowing rival centers of authority; what is more, they tend to extend their oppression over other peoples, and have historically shown themselves to be less susceptible to liberalization than authoritarian regimes—Greece, Portugal and Spain are examples of democratic evolution without parallel in the Communist world.

For these reasons, the threat to individual liberty and world peace arising from totalitarian states appears to the current administration to be greater than that posed by authoritarian countries. This, the current administration argues, does not confer approval on the practices of authoritarian dictators; it indicates, however, the administration's feeling that it is appropriate to single out human rights violations in Communist countries because of their unique "permanency, aggressiveness and brutality."[186]

Even abhorrence for totalitarian regimes, however, would not itself justify a more severe human rights policy with regard to these countries. The factor that makes totalitarian regimes this administration's major concern is the seeming willingness of the Soviet Union and its proxies to violate international boundaries to extend their influence. According to this view, the Soviet Union and the regimes it supports are little better than "conspiracies masquerading as states," which abet terrorists to further their aims. Some evidence has accumulated during the Carter and Reagan administrations to support this conclusion,[187] and the current administration claims that its focus on terrorism shows its concern not only with human rights violations of governments, but also with such violations committed by opposition groups. "Terrorism," concludes the most recently released human rights country report, "has an intrinsic tendency to corrode the very basis of human rights; accordingly, United States policy includes a serious effort to control it."[188]

To Reagan's critics, singling out totalitarian regimes threatens to make the policy merely a lopsided criticism of the Soviet Union and its allies. They fear that the human rights policy will lose credibility if it loses its evenhandedness. Spokesmen for the administration counter that they are trying to restore evenhandedness after the Carter administration's single minded concentration on human rights violations among Latin American countries and some of our allies. The new administration feels it will restore greater credibility to the policy by redirecting blame toward those whose rights violations are the most serious. In a scathing attack on the "double standard" applied to human rights, Ambassador Jeane J. Kirkpatrick lashed out at the United Nations where, she claims, "moral outrage is distributed much like violence in a protection racket,"[189] adding that "no aspect of UN affairs has become more perverted by politicization than have its human rights activities" and that human rights have "become a bludgeon to be wielded by the strong against the weak, by the majority against the isolated, by the blocs against the unorganized."[190]

The Reagan administration accordingly seeks to restore "evenhandedness" in U.S. dealings with human rights and to exert its influence toward shifting international institutions away from their "double standard" by encouraging regional solutions to international human rights concerns.[191]

Having labelled the enemies of human rights, what positive alternatives does the Reagan administration offer? Which human rights are we as a country sworn to defend? Surely it is not enough to say that we are opposed to the spread of totalitarianism. Former National Security Advisor Richard Allen was one of the first to address this issue publicly:

> Human rights in the proper sense of the term are the rights guaranteed to men under law in any civilized or human society. These include, most fundamentally, the rights not to be deprived arbitrarily of life, liberty or property, and the rights not to be subjected to humanly degrading treatment such as torture or exile under brutal conditions. . . .[192]

The significance of civil and political rights are duly noted in this passage, but another category of rights emphasized by former president Carter—economic and social rights—is wholly missing. The current administration argues that the notion of economic and social rights "is a dilution and distortion of the original and proper meaning of human rights."[193] Ambassador Kirkpatrick has almost questioned the motives of those who advance socio-economic rights alongside civil and political rights:

> . . . an effort has been mounted to deprive the concept of human rights of specific meaning by pretending that all objects of human desire are "rights" which can be had, if not for the asking, then at least for the demanding. The proliferation of "rights"—to a happy childhood, to self-fulfillment, to development—has proceeded at the same time that the application of human rights standards has grown more distorted and more cynical.[194]

Reagan's officials moreover, feel that the extension of socioeconomic rights is often used merely to justify internal repression. "It serves," said Richard Allen, "as a convenient excuse for those regimes and movements which do not respect ordinary civil and political rights; not surprisingly, it has been taken up by the Soviet Union and its allies and surrogates as a way to defend the dismal human rights record of most communist governments."[195]

Not acknowledging a right simply because it might be distorted or exploited, however, is no reason to say that such a right does not exist. A more subtle argument against socio-economic rights could be that, as currently propounded, socio-economic rights presuppose a large measure of government intervention and income redistribution within and between nations. Not surprisingly, in light of its domestic policies, the current administration has rejected this argument as unjustifiable and as the worst possible way of improving socio-economic conditions for the world's poor. In his speech on the "Right to Development" before the United Nations Human Rights Commission, Michael Novak seemed to place freedom of enterprise alongside other essential political freedoms, while coming to the defense of much maligned transnational corporations:

> Mr. Chairman, we have heard distinguished delegates in this room speak of "obscene profits." Are we to understand that losses are virtuous? Where there are not profits, there can be only losses or stagnation. But these are the exact opposite of development. Development itself is a form of profit. . . . A reasonable rate of return is just; a reasonable amount of losses must, in some years, be expected but, on the whole, an economy without profit is an economy without development.[196]

Novak further notes that economic freedom has often led to political freedom in authoritarian regimes, hence the deathly fear totalitarian regimes have of letting their economies breathe freely.[197]

Such discussion according to Elliott Abrams, the current Assistant Secretary of State for Human Rights and Humanitarian Affairs, is not meant to slight the unquestionable "urgency and moral seriousness of the need to eliminate starvation and poverty from the world . . . ," but only to stress that, in this administration's view, "no category of rights should be allowed to become an excuse for the denial of other rights" and that the best ways of establishing civil liberties and economic prosperity is to unleash the forces of the marketplace.[198] Interestingly, in its most authoritative formulation, the administration never explicitly denies that social or economic needs may be considered rights; rather it feels that at the present time the idea is too easily abused and too ill-conceived to be useful.

The Reagan administration has unfortunately allowed its ideology to outdistance concrete policy proposals in this crucial area. It has not accepted the view of some conservative critics of the previous administration, like Adda Bozeman, that socio-economic rights, because they are in a different category than civil and political rights, might be more properly approached through legislation. It has also alienated much of the Third World by appearing unconcerned with issues of social justice which many Third World leaders unabashedly consider of paramount importance.

The current administration has said it wishes to propose to the world an "American" human rights philosophy. This is somewhat understandable, given the tendency among other major blocs such as the Socialist countries and the Lesser Developed Nations, to be equally dogmatic about the definition of human rights. It is essential, consequently, that our human rights philosophy be well defined. Human rights is intrinsically a concept that transcends national boundaries. It is important, therefore, that some measure of agreement be reached on a universal definition of human rights. The United States need not always agree with the ideologically motivated positions popular in the United Nations General Assembly, but Reagan's prolonged uncertainty about socio-economic rights greatly weakens our ability to present a credible and coherent American stance on human rights and only further diminishes the chances of arriving at a universally acceptable definition of human rights.

POLICY IMPLEMENTATION UNDER REAGAN

Each new administration likes to put its own imprint on existing policies. This is especially true of the Reagan administration which took over and transformed some of the human rights mechanisms set up by Jimmy Carter. It was widely assumed that since the new President had been so critical of Carter's human rights policy, he would drastically reduce its scope, perhaps even abolish it entirely. President Reagan's first nominee to head Humanitarian Affairs, Ernest W. Lefever, certainly did not reassure human rights supporters. The policy having been congressionally mandated, however, a new president is faced with constraints in his choice of options, and whether it was the original intent of the Reagan team, or whether they quickly learned the limits of their influence, it appears that certain reforms of the human rights bureau undertaken by this administration have helped more than hurt the bureau.

Not surprisingly, there was a large turnover of senior officials at Humanitarian Affairs when Reagan became Prresident. Some, like Warren Christopher, had already expressed a desire to return to private life after four years no matter what the outcome of the elections. Others had been mentioned as subject to replacement even if Carter were reelected. Many political appointees left with the advent of the new administration. Perhaps more startling to some is the fact that several senior career officials were kept on. Stephen E. Palmer, Jr. a career diplomat who acceded to Mark Schneider's job in 1978, and who since that time has directed the compilation of the bureau's country reports (including the 1981 report issued by this administration), was appointed Acting Assistant Secretary of State for Human Rights and Humanitarian Affairs. He held that job until December 1981 and remained on in the bureau until March 1982. To an extent, in the persons of senior officials like Stephen Palmer, Theresa Tull and others, continuity was fostered.

Late in the Carter administration, it became clear that a large scale re-organization would be necessary to improve the bureau's effectiveness. Indeed, the bureau had been in the throes of constant renovation and restructuring since its inception. In 1979 refugee affairs mushroomed, becoming too large to tuck away inside Humanitarian Affairs and was transferred. It was also debated whether security assistance should be given a special office in the bureau and one was temporarily opened. But, plans for a major functional and geographic reorganization were undertaken by Carter and are being completed under Reagan. Currently, the Office of Human Rights within the Bureau has five area officers, one for each continent, to survey human rights conditions in their areas. In addition, there is a functional officer dealing with arms transfers, as well as an economic officer dealing with trade issues. Finally, there is a full-time liaison to various non-governmental organizations, as well as an office for overall policy and planning headed by Charles Fairbanks. When this reorganization is completed, the bureau is expected to have four to five people more than it had under Carter, a fact indicative of the bureau's importance when one keeps in mind this administration's zest for budget slashing.

More often than not, however, congressional and other critics have accused the President of curtailing bureau activities. An instance often cited is the demise of the Interagency Group on Human Rights and Foreign Assistence, often referred to as the Christopher Group. It should be noted, however, that in this action Reagan did not depart from his predecessor's policies. The Christopher Group was formed to coordinate policies and to educate concerned agencies about human rights. During the Carter administration's last years in office, when the procedure for human rights reviews had become fairly routine, the original group met less and less frequently, since the educative function had elapsed and other issues could usually be resolved at the staff level. The full Interagency Group met thirteen times its first year, but only. nine times in 1978, five times in 1979, and twice in 1980.[199] The actual human rights review shifted to a working group headed by the Economic and Business Bureau at the State Department and the Economic Office of HA, which included director level representatives of various agencies. The working group met twice a month during the year to formulate budget requests and, if a disagreement over a certain country arose, rather than convening the entire Interagency Group, it became customary to submit the dispute in an action memorandum to Warren Christopher for a personal decision.

The process has continued under the Reagan administration, with regular reviews by the working group. In view of Secretary Haig's relative disinterest in human rights matters, it was William P. ("Judge") Clark who oversaw human rights matters. Although he is credited with having been the primary author of the State Department memorandum on human rights,[200] Clark saw his role at the State Department more as one of a liaison to the President, rather than of being involved in elaborating State Department policy. Decisions on controversial human rights matters therefore fell to then Under Secretary of State for Political Affairs Walter J. Stoessel, Jr. and following him, to Lawrence Eagleburger, who has continued to supervise after Clark's transfer to the National Security Council.

While the actual procedures for human rights review has been inherited from the last years of the Carter administration, it is nonetheless true that the Reagan administration has implanted a different spirit concerning human rights in the existing institutions. Undoubtedly, for example, Secretary Haig and his staff were much less accessible to HA officials than Cyrus Vance was. Vance and Derian had informal meetings at least once each week; moreover, human rights was known to be of vital concern to the President. Within the department Carter appointees were perceived as concerned, tenacious, sometimes even pushy in their concern for human rights. The current human rights team views the boisterous approach, although perhaps necessary at that time, as being less productive now that the world has gotten the message that the U.S. intends to pursue a human rights policy. Coupled with this, naturally, is the personal imprimatur of Ronald Reagan, who strongly believes that our security needs have been neglected in the past and that we need to give first priority to defense. Translated into human rights terms, this means a stronger concern in HA about the need to prevent nations strategically important to us from turning Communist.

This administration has grouped internationally recognized rights into two categories: 1) the right to be free from government violations of integrity, and 2) the right to civil and political liberties.[201] In applying policy to principle, administration spokesmen have said they would be concerned with several criteria: the effectiveness of the policy, its results, the egregiousness of and persistence of human rights violations, our capacity to influence events, the larger context of our strategic responsibilities, and preventing the spread of totalitarianism.[202]

Another related principle is that human rights cannot be divorced from American security considerations and must therefore be integrated into our foreign policy:

> We believe that human rights are not only compatible with our national interest; they are an indispensible element of the American approach—at home and abroad. Our objective is to make our security interests and our human rights concerns mutually reinforcing so that they can be pursued in tandem.[203]

It is also understood that America's human rights standards must be applied without prejudice across the board. As former Secretary of State Haig affirmed at an address before the OAS General Assembly, "We should not be more tolerant of the infraction of those who reject democratic values and peaceful change yet more critical of the lapses of those searching for democracy and social justice."[204] This fairness must also extend to international bodies, which have electively applied human rights sanctions to pro-Western countries while ignoring Communist atrocities. Fairness, argue Reagan human rights spokesmen, dictates that this administration seek to redress this imbalance by stressing neglected human rights abuses. Thus, "it is a significant service to the cause of human rights to limit the influence the USSR (together with its clients and proxies) can exert . . . [by bringing] Soviet bloc violations to the attention of the world over and over again."[205]

A frequent criticism voiced by Carter administration human rights activists was that "traditional diplomacy" was not concerned with the future course of events and how these would affect American interests. The human rights policy was their alternative. Like its predecessor, the Reagan adminisration points to the human rights policy as an illustration of its concern for long-term American interests. As opposed to the previous administration, however, it does not generally assume that changes in the status quo will result in an improvement in human rights conditions. Thus, Elliott Abrams recently urged Congress not to withdraw aid to the government of El Salvador becuase the alternative to the current regime could be worse:

> In Vietnam, in Nicaragua, in Iran, we were told that the government we supported was corrupt and oppressive and that the other side was the progressive side and would respect democracy. We were told that human rights would gain if the other side won. We now hear this argument again about El

Salvador. . . . This in my view is blindness. How many times must we learn this lesson?

We want to be very sure that in a situation such as El Salvador, we do not trade the serious but solvable human rights problems of today for a permanent Communist dictatorship. Resisting the expansion of communism is a key human rights goal.[207]

There are a variety of levers this administration uses to indicate American displeasure over human rights violations. If relations with the country are not friendly, the Reagan administration prefers to initiate discussions privately, much like the Carter administration. There is, however, under Reagan a definite deemphasizing of public criticism of our allies and of countries strategically significant to us, and greater willingness to criticize Communist countries publicly. This tendency reflects the ideological proclivities of the Reagan presidency, but it also reflects a very pragmatic political reality; according to this administration, the United States has much more influence over countries with whom it trades extensively. With these countries quiet diplomacy is more credible and more effective. Our economic leverage over the socialist countries on the other hand is extremely limited; therefore, public criticism is usually the only resort.

For Reagan, moreover, there is no need to "scream human rights" from the housetops domestically because our government already embodies these principles. Some, like Ernest W. Lefever, see the very notion of a separate bureau for dealing with human rights as redundant, the presumption being that it is only natural for American foreign policy to be concerned with human rights. Delegating supervisory responsibility for human rights to a single bureau, they argue, might produce an effect opposite to that desired. Other bureaus might relinquish their responsibility for considering human rights entirely human rights bureau. Whether or not the government took human rights considerations adequately into account before the creation of the Bureau for Human Rights and Humanitarian Affairs (HA)—an assertion which the Carter human rights people flatly reject—subsequent experience suggests that the creation of an independent rights bureau has led other bureaus and agencies to leave with HA the thankless task of dealing with human rights issues.

In the rhetoric of human rights, both those supporting the policy and those against it seem to assume that there are two approaches to dealing with human rights abuses: public or private. In reality there has been only one approach, combining the two. The difference between the Carter and Reagan policies on this point has again been one of emphasis, not ideology. The Reagan administration has propagandized human rights violations less than its predecessor, for it does not see drawing world attention to abuses as the primary objective:

> The problem is what we do about awareness. And here is where effective quiet diplomacy, sometimes supplemented by public pronouncements and coordinated with international organizations, can make a difference in lifting the burden of brutality from human beings and extending the range of freedom and human dignity. [208]

In choosing the instruments for implementing the human rights policy, Elliott Abrams argues, the United States government should be guided primarily by the

> *criterion of effectiveness,* choosing the response that is most likely to actually improve human rights. The most effective means, generally, is traditional diplomacy which maximizes the limited leverage we do possess, while minimizing counterproductive reactions, damage to bilateral relations and international tension. Traditional diplomacy has the drawback of being least visible precisely where it is most successful. But this Administration is pledged to employ traditional diplomacy vigorously on behalf of human rights. [209]

Traditional diplomacy, according to Walter J. Stoessel, Jr., requires the combination of public and private diplomacy. [210]

If human rights abuses are not corrected through diplomatic initiatives, the government has several ways it could go public: through the State Department, through the Congress, through private interest groups, and through increasing use of international bodies.

The failure of the economic "carrot and stick" has been observed by officials in both administrations. Despite "Harkin language" only a modest shifting of funds within the foreign aid budget attributable to human rights consideration. President Reagan has therefore been reluctant to curtail aid as a lever for inducing compliance with human rights standards, arguing that total disengagement, say in the case of El Salvador, would be an abandonment of our commitment to human rights. According to Elliott Abrams, such a move might have "the immediate advantage of distancing ourselves from the abusers. We just walk away. It looks easy, and it looks like a quick low-cost option."[211] But, it is fraught with greater perils for the future stability of the region. This argument is also used to justify the administration's strengthened ties to the repressive regimes of South Africa and South Korea:

> It is our view that isolating these countries, driving them away from us, would do nothing but decrease our influence there. Our ability to obtain our goals, including our human rights goals, is sufficient only when America is understood to be an important force.[212]

More effective has been the potential threat of withdrawal of American support, particularly in regional development banks. More than one country has withdrawn a loan from consideration as a result of such a threat.

The most significant difference between the two administrations has been this reading of the language of statute 116 e. For Elliott Abrams the reference in the law to a "consistent pattern of gross violations" indicates that if such a pattern has ceased and conditions appear to be improving, this warrants United States support. For Patricia Derian this is a misreading of the law. If any human rights violation continues to occur, she argues, the United States is obligated to seek their rectification. In subsequent testimony administration officials have acknowledged that absolute human rights conditions must also affect our policies, but trends are nonetheless "weighed carefully."[213]

Because of existing statutes, similarities inevitably persist between the Reagan and Carter human rights policies despite the philosophical differences. Another factor enhancing continuity between the two administrations is the apparent deemphasizing of the totalitarian versus authoritarian dichotomy that figured so prominently in the initial statements of Reagan appointees. The first indication of this came in the June 1981 testimony before the House of Representatives of Walter J. Stoessel, Jr. who, in his prepared statement, did not once mention this distinction. The text of his speech, given before two subcommitees, reflected a reassessment and had been cleared "at the appropriately high level," according to one administration official. Since then the State Department has entirely dropped the usage of these terms, deeming them too confusing and difficult to explain. Importantly, though they have been dropped by the State Department, they have not been discarded by all administration officials (most notably Jeane J. Kirkpatrick), and there is little doubt that this dichotomy, so fundamental to Reagan's worldview, persists among his key appointees.

Like their counterparts under Carter, spokesmen for human rights in this administration would like to see their task eventually shift from concentrating on individual cases to dealing with governmental policies themselves. With president Reagan in office the change has been more one of style than substance. Human rights spokesmen for the previous administration at times seemed oblivious of the necessities of getting along with the world; by contrast, the current administration is careful not to put human rights in a category by itself. "Practically speaking," warned former Secretary of State Alexander Haig, "policy on human rights must be integrated into the sphere of diplomacy, not pursued as if it were the only virtue in a foreign policy of otherwise petty or distasteful acts."[214]

Yet, integrating human rights into "traditional diplomacy," as is Reagan's objective, demands a functional dichotomy within the policy. Elliott Abrams was very clear on this point when he said that, beyond responding to individual violations we must have a "second track of positive policy with a bolder long-term aim: to assist the gradual emergence of free political systems."[215] How are we to accomplish this? Through our support of stable institutions of popular government abroad. This view is premised on the example of our own history according to Ambassador Jeane J. Kirkpatrick:

> . . . the freedom of the American people was based not on the marvelous and inspiring slogans of Thomas Paine but on the careful web of restraint and permission and interests and traditions which was woven by our founding fathers into the Constitution and explained in the Federalist Papers . . .[216]

Human rights are made real through institutions of popular government, what Michael Novak has called the "active, free, organized, and competitive interests under due process. . . . The test of human rights, therefore, lies not in words. The test of human rights lies in the functioning of institutions of free association, free speech, open and organized public dissent."[217] Consequently, the administration's premise has been to bolster human rights by building up institutions of due process and free associations of individuals in all countries around the world. "The development of liberty," says Abrams, is "encouraged by the emergence of areas within a political system where free choice and free expression can become familiar and respected. . . ."; what President Reagan recently called "the infrastructure of democracy."[218]

WHITHER HUMAN RIGHTS?

The United States has always, consciously or unconsciously, pursued some form of human rights policy. After all, this country came into existence by establishing a political order and set of principles based on human rights and unique in its day. It cannot help but express these convictions in its foreign policy. Human rights are, therefore, not a new concern for this government; nor is the debate over how to best express our human rights concerns to other countries new. What is novel is our preoccupation with human rights since the early seventies, and particularly the attempt by some to transform a domestic aspiration—that respect for human rights might some day become universal—into a crusade, the Western equivalent of Communist ideology. Judge Thomas Buergenthal, a noted spokesman for human rights, was recently quoted as saying:

> In today's world, ideology is as much a weapon as is sophisticated weaponry. A sound human rights policy provides the United States with an ideology that distinguishes us most clearly from the Soviet Union and seriously undercuts the ideological appeal of communism. It is the only ideology, the only dream, if you will, that the people of the United States shares with the majority of people of the—Second and Third Worlds.[219]

Warren Christopher, former Deputy Secretary of State and the State Department official primarily responsible for the human rights policy under President Carter recently concurred that "our human rights policy . . . identifies the United States with leaders around the world who are trying to improve the lot of their people. . . . It gives us a way of taking the ideological initiative, instead of merely reacting."[220]

Ideology, however, is an imperfect substitute for policy. The above statements contain two aspects of the current human rights debate which need to be distinguished. One, is the search for the appropriate philosophy of human rights describing a worldview to which United States foreign policy must make reference. This worldview ought never become an ideology, however, which by implication would make it a doctrinaire set of assumptions meant to explain all of reality and the future. So interpreted, our human rights policy would indeed become the equivalent of Communist ideology, but it would also spell the end of either a credible human rights policy or a credible foreign policy.

The second aspect of a viable human rights policy deals with implementation. Here discussion has focused largely on the amount of leverage our policies have on improving human rights conditions in other countries. True, our human rights policy invariably influences the behavior of other nations, primarily because it is espoused by the United States government rather than for its intrinsic merit, but we must bear in mind that such influence is limited and varies from country to country. Since our ability to influence regimes and our own interests abroad range widely, strict equality in implementing a human rights policy is neither possible nor desirable; however, we have no justification for this difference other than healthy self-interest, a motive some will find inherently unsatisfactory.

The stated objective of this administration is to integrate human rights into the broader framework of our entire foreign policy. This would appear to be a commendable aim. It places human rights alongside our other foreign policy objectives where it can be compared and judged on its merits. At the same time, however, this creates a problem. As President Carter and Patricia Derian found out, there is no inherent constituency in our foreign policy establishment that supports human rights, so that more often than not human rights are in contravention of other vested interests. By placing human rights on equal grounds rather than constantly emphasizing it, one runs the risk of having it overlooked.

Another criticism applied to the Reagan administration is that placing human rights totally within the ambit of our foreign policy has tended to blur the distinctions between human rights and other national security issues. Although there is perhaps some connection between human rights and terrorism, and human rights and the prevention of nuclear war, one sometimes wonders if, by emphasizing broader policy, this administration has not overlooked individual human rights violations, which have come to be generally identified with the term human rights. Indeed, by subsuming human rights totally to American foreign policy, one can justify almost any foreign policy initiative as an act supportive of human rights, thus damaging both the credibility of our policies and the integrity of the concept of human rights. A human rights policy of the United States government should certainly be guided by our national and security interests. At the same time, however, it must reflect commonly held assumptions about the nature of human rights to be worthy of the name.

It should also give us pause that history has not always shown our influence to be beneficial. As with any policy when it shifts from paper to practice, there are examples where the singular pursuit of human rights has worsened the human rights situation in a country or done damage to other American interests. Our loss of influence in Latin America, accompanied by the anger of several heads of state in that region is one example; another is Ethiopia's switch to Soviet arms and aid following our blunt criticism of human rights violations in that region. Part of the reason our efforts abroad have not been very successful has been the selective withholding of foreign assistance. Judged at the time to be the most effective tool we could wield to ensure compliance with human rights standards, it has since proved to be a blunt and double edged weapon. It is therefore imperative to search for other, more practical, means of influencing foreign countries. The Reagan administration's stress on institutions is one such innovation which, while not as dramatic as the cut-off of aid, has the advantage of being less ephemeral and more difficult to repeal once implemented. It also presupposes accommodation with and respect for the institutional processes of other countries.

Human rights followed a two-track policy under both administrations: one, the immediate response to current violations; second, the construction of a long-term human rights framework that would prevent such violations from reocurring. Carter administration officials tended to view the transition from the immediate to the long-term as relatively imminent and had faith that the United Nations would ultimately serve as international monitor of human rights. The Reagan administration has been more sanguine about constructing an international framework for human rights. It has stressed the need to reform domestic institutions and reliance on regional human rights organizations rather than on the United Nations alone. It has also been more mindful, perhaps as a result of President Carter's experience, of the way in which the immediate goals of the human rights policy can conflict with its long-term agenda. One example is the manner in which United States intervention in support of noted Soviet dissidents lcd to a harsh crackdown on other dissidents. The severe crackdown on the Soviet dissident community over the past few years can, in large part, be attributed to its increasing international prominence. Although the effects of public criticism of one government by another are impossible to trace, the negative effects of this case seem to indicate that quiet diplomacy may be of greater use in raising most human rights issues, and that public opprobrium should be reserved for extremely severe, life-threatening violations.

Furthermore, if one accepts the current administration's point that some qualitative distinction between totalitarian and authoritarian regimes ought to be made, it becomes easier to distinguish the objectives of our human rights policy in these two groups of countries. In authoritarian regimes, Reagan supporters argue, human rights violations are not endemic to the regime but to a specific ruling cabal. Totalitarian rulers, on the other hand, often find it difficult to distinguish simple criticism from outright rebellion. To make this dichotomy effective requires that American human rights policy be flexible enough to pursue different tactics in authoritarian and totalitarian countries within the framework of a global strategy to enhance human rights. In authoritarian countries, where a certain number of independent institutions already exist, these ought to be helped to expand their influence. Authoritarian governments sould also be encouraged to view internal criticism as legitimate and constructive.

An entirely different set of problems face human rights issues in totalitarian regions. The lack of alternative sources of authority has transformed the governmental structure there into a topheavy pyramid which, if seriously threatened, could collapse the entire country into chaos. The first task of an effective human rights policy in these areas would thus be to encourage the formation of alternative sources of authority to which the populace could appeal for redress of their grievances if ignored by their government. Although this at first appears to be a long-range goal, it can also be viewed as a cumulative process that begins in the present. Trade sanctions will always be of limited success against countries that have little trade with the United States. Furthermore, compliance with human rights can ultimately be assumed only by the domestic authorities. Hence, we see in the Soviet Union the formation of "watch groups" to monitor the government's compliance with human rights and the creation of the semi-underground trade union SMOT, active since 1979. A vivid example of this process is before us in Poland, where the trade union movement and the Catholic Church are already seen as alternative sources of authority. In every country, whether authoritarian, totalitarian, or democratic, it is essential to foster what President Reagan has termed, "the infrastructure of democracy—the system of a free press, unions, political parties, universities—which allows a people to choose their own way, to develop their own culture, to reconcile their own differences through peaceful means."[221] This pursuit at times bring us into conflict with other nations, but it is essential to human rights and plays a not indifferent role to our own security.

The conflict between America's human rights objectives and our other foreign policy aims is also accentuated by the fact that our current human rights policy combines two disparate functions: that of external critic of all international human rights violations, and that of policy decisionmaking on the issue of human rights. What may be termed a "conflict of interest" ensues whereby, as an agency of the United States government dealing with other sovereign states, our human rights bureau cannot allow itself the same liberty to criticize human rights violations that an independent agency could. To argue otherwise would place us in the unenviable position of being the self-appointed judge of international human rights, with predictable consequences for our relations with other countries. It would mean divorcing human rights from international relations, thereby sharply decreasing its effectiveness. Human rights absolutists have criticized both the Carter and the Reagan administrations for their silence. They in fact argue for a separation between the roles of criticism and policy-making, since a responsible human rights policy must take the welfare and security of the American people into account. It cannot jeopardize our relations with *any* country solely on the basis of human rights considerations or it could not rightly be called a human rights policy *of the United States government,* whose primary responsibility it is to ensure the peace and security of the people of *this* country.

There is considerable truth in the observation of British columnist Ferdinand Mount that "governments by their nature cannot consistently put human rights first for the simple reason that it is the existence of the nation state that creates 'the human rights problem' in the first place."[222] It is wiser, under these circumstances, to modify our human rights policy than to attempt to modify the international system of nation states.

For those who equate U.S. human rights policy with domestic and international morality this may be an intolerable situation, but we might ask ourselves what are the alternatives? Are we prepared as a country to expend the effort necessary to modify the current system of nation states to another more to our liking? Should we risk alienating allies as well as enemies? Should we heighten international tensions further by adding to the panoply of causes already cluttering the international arena? Our human rights policy alone, contrary to what some may say, is not what distinguishes us from the Soviet Union; it is only one visible sign of a philosophy and political tradition that is !he antithesis of Communist totalitarianism. Our own observance of human rights stems from this tradition, so why should we assume the inverse will be true of other countries? Without the support of adequate institutions of self-government and a pluralistic political philosophy, human rights stand little chance of establishing themselves anywhere.

Human rights should, furthermore, not be loosely equated with morality. Whatever the morality of our conduct in foreign affairs, it does not stem from the comparatively narrow concept of human rights. In fact, the two should be carefully distinguished, for it invites only confusion and self-righteousness to equate human rights, or any other policy of the United States government, with morality.

By skirting the pitfalls and charting our course carefully in relation to all the other stars in the universe of foreign policy concerns, there is still a vital role for human rights to play in our foreign policy. Foreign policy does not intrinsically deal with making the world a better place. Dissatisfaction with the results of our policies can stem not only from an ideological bent, but from a review of recent events. Conservatives and liberals alike, for example, criticize America's response to the crises in Hungary, Cuba, Vietnam and Angola (for differing reasons to be sure). Both are fully aware that what happened was probably not the best possible outcome. Human rights in this sense provide a point of orientation in searching for responses that make for a better world.

In a recent article, Jeane J. Kirkpatrick queried, "It feels good to be good, but is this good foreign policy?"[223] The answer, obviously, is no, but neither is it good foreign policy to feel bad. Within the confines of what is possible without seriously damaging American interests, realizing that international change will proceed slowly and not always in the direction we desire, we ought to pursue a policy of human rights. Not only will this make us feel better, our tradition demands it, and we as a people demand it of our government.

Moreover, human rights helps to bridge the gap between domestic and international concerns. In this regard Carter's advisers come closer to the truth than those of Reagan. The latter still cling to the dictum that our foreign policy must deal primarily with the foreign policies of other nations, not their domestic policies, as if country's foreign policy were not the product of its domestic affairs. The explosion of international trade and telecommunications has drastically eroded this barrier. This is not to say that national sovereignty can be disregarded; it is still much the dominant force in the system of nation states. It is, as yet, primarily through respect for sovereignty that we are able to influence domestic events. Nonetheless, the fact that human rights appears to be generally recognized as an issue that transcends borders and links domestic and international issues should not be forgotten.

The international system under which we live severely limits options for change. A human rights policy would be easier to implement under an empire, such as that of Charlemagne or the Romans. Today it is more problematic and, in the future, depending on our actions, it could become either more or less difficult. Our situation, however, is never static. Even on the fringes of interstate relations, where current international practice places human rights, policies like that of human rights have an impact in shaping the present and the future of international relations. We should use these moral opportunities at the fringes with creative enthusiasm and the utmost vigor, seeking constantly to expand them. This requires patience, postponed gratification, and realism. Progress will not always be steady, and at times there will be setbacks due to overzealousness and misjudgement, but in the long run, pursuing a human rights policy that is guided by prudence should allow us to leave the world a better place than we entered it.

ENDNOTES

1. Peter G. Brown and Douglas Maclean, eds., *Human Rights and U.S. Foreign Policy* (Lexington, Mass.: Lexington Books, 1979), 3.
2. Charles Frankel, *Human Rights and Foreign Policy,* Headline Series 241 (New York: Foreign Policy Association, October 1978), 3.
3. *Ibid.,* 11.
4. Donald P. Kommers and Gilbert D. Loescher, eds., *Human Rights and American Foreign Policy* (Notre Dame, Ind.: University of Notre Dame, 1979), 263.
5. M. Glen Johnson, "Historical Perspectives on Human Rights and U.S. Foreign Policy," *Universal Human Rights* 2 (July-September 1980): 2. 6. *Ibid.,* 3. This passage has often been cited by foreign policy spokesmen like George F. Kennan, Ernest W. Lefever, and others who have argued for greater circumspection in the pursuit of our ideals.
7. Sandy Vogelgesang, *American Dreams, Global Nightmares* (New York: Norton, 1980), 73.
8. Kommers and Loescher, *Human Rights,* 258.
9. Johnson, "Historical Perspectives," 5.
10. Vogelgesang, *American Dreams,* 73.
11. Kenneth W. Thompson, ed. *The Moral Imperative of Human Rights* (Washington, D.C.: Univ. Press of America, 1980), 45.
12. Johnson, "Historical Perspectives," 13.
13. John Lewis Gaddis, *The United States and the Origins of the Cold War, 1941-1947* (New York: Columbia, 1972), 11.
14. Johnson, "Historical Perspectives," 14.
15. Patricia Weiss Fagen, "The United States and International Human Rights, 1946-1977," *Universal Human Rights* 2 (July-September 1980): 25.
16. *The Washington Post.* 5 February 1979, A 17.

17. Kommers and Loescher, *Human Rights*, 217.
18. *Ibid.*, 221.
19. Brown and Maclean, *Human Rights*, 178.
20. *Human Rights in United States and United Kingdom Foreign Policy: A Colloquium*, held at Palace of Westminster, November 27-28, 1978 (New York: American Assoc. for the Int'l. Commission of Jurists, 1979), 8; also Brown and Maclean, 98.
21. Brown and Maclean, *Human Rights*, 4.
22. *Ibid.*, 4-5.
23. *Ibid.*, 5.
24. *Ibid.*, 6.
25. *Ibid.*
26. Vogelgesang, *American Dreams*, 143.
27. *Ibid.*
28. Kommers and Loescher, *Human Rights*, 11.
29. Vogelgesang, *American Dreams*, 127.
30. Kommers and Loescher, *Human Rights*, 22.
31. Vogelgesang, *American Dreams*, 127.
32. Brown and Maclean, *Human Rights*, 57.
33. *Ibid.*, 7.
34. *Ibid.*, 8.
35. Vogelgesang, *American Dreams*, 134-35.
36. Brown and Maclean, *Human Rights*, 9.
37. Thompson, *Moral Imperatives*, 51.
38. Vogelgesang, *American Dreams*, 141.
39. *Ibid.*, 141-42.
40. Hoyt Gimlin, ed., *U.S. Foreign Policy*, Editorial Research Reports (Washington, D.C.: Congressional Quarterly, 1979), 6.
41. Vogelgesang, *American Dreams*, 138, 140.
42. *Human Rights and U.S. Foreign Assistance*, a report prepared for the Committee on Foreign Relations, U.S. Senate, by the Congressional Research Service, 96th Cong., 1st Session (November, 1979), 1. [hereafter: *Foreign Assistance*]
43. Patricia M. Derian, "Human Rights and American Foreign Policy," *Universal Human Rights* 1 (January-March 1979): 6.
44. *Ibid.*, 3.
45. *Ibid.*
46. Vogelgesang, *American Dreams*, 108.
47. Derian, "Human Rights," 4.
48. David P. Forsythe, "American Foreign Policy and Human Rights," *Universal Human Rights* 2 (July-September 1980), 39.

49. *Foreign Assistance*, 69.
50. *The New York Times*, 18 March 1977, A 10.
51. *The New York Times*, 9 February 1977.
52. *The New York Times*, 2 February 1977, 12 June 1977, 1.
53. *The New York Times*, 1 July 1977, A 10, 23 May 1977, 12.
54. *The New York Times*, 23 May 1977, 12.
55. Vogelgesang, *American Dreams*, 141.
56. *Ibid.*
57. A. Glenn Mower, *The United States, The United Nations, and Human Rights* (Westport, Conn.: Greenwood Press, 1979), 87.
58. B. G. Ramcharan, *Human Rights* (The Hague: Martinus Hijhoff, 1979), 28.
59. Vogelgesang, *American Dreams*, 122.
60. Brown and Maclean, *Human Rights*, 199-200.
61. *Ibid.*, 15; also Vogelgesang, 47.
62. Brown and Maclean, *Human Rights*, 18.
63. Forsythe, "American Foreign Policy," 40.
64. Mower, *United States*, 140.
65. Gimlin, U.S. *Foreign Policy*, 6.
66. Vogelgesang, *American Dreams*, 47.
67. *Ibid.*, 245.
68. *Ibid.*, 82.
69. *Ibid.*, 87.
70. Brown and Maclean, *Human Rights*, 16-17.
71. Vogelgesang, *American Dreams*, 75.
72. *Ibid.*, 84.
73. *Ibid.*, 85.
74. *Ibid.*, 83.
75. *Ibid.*, 79.
76. Mower, *United States*, 102.
77. Kommers and Loescher, *Human Rights*, 239-40.
78. *Human Rights in . . .* , 48, 53.
79. Mower, *United States*, 53, 119.
80. *Ibid.*, 102.
81. Johnson, "Historical Perspectives," 17.
82. *The Los Angeles Times*, 11 December 1977.
83. Vogelgesang, *American Dreams*, 80.
84. Brown and Maclean, *Human Rights*, 213.
85. *Ibid.*, 207-08
86. *Foreign Assistance*, 1-2.
87. *Ibid.*, 52-53.
88. *Ibid.*, 69.
89. *Ibid.*, 37.

90. *Ibid.,* 19.
91. *Ibid.,* 52-53.
92. Gimlin, U.S. Foreign Policy, 12.
93. *Foreign Assistance,* 36-37.
94. *Ibid.,* 37-38.
95. *Ibid.,* 38.
96. *Ibid.,* 39.
97. *Ibid.,* 38.
98. Kommers and Loescher, *Human Rights,* 219.
99. *Ibid.,* 226; also *Foreign Assistance,* 22.
100. Barry M. Rubin and Elizabeth P. Spiro, eds., *Human Rights and U.S. Foreign Policy* (Boulder, CO: Westview Press, 1979), 35.
101. Kommers and Loescher, *Human Rights,* 231.
102. Thompson, *Moral Imperatives,* 53.
103. Kommers and Loescher, *Human Rights,* 233.
104. *Foreign Assistance,* 31.
105. Vogelgesang, *American Dreams,* 60.
106. Mower, *United States,* 118.
107. *Foreign Assistance,* 33.
108. *Ibid.,* 43.
109. *Ibid.,* 44.
110. *Foreign Assistance,* 45. A similar stipulation regarding South Africa has been in effect since 1962.
111. *Ibid.,* 40.
112. *Ibid.,* 19.
113. *Ibid.,* 41.
114. *Ibid.,* 33.
115. Derian, "Human Rights," 8-9.
116. *Foreign Assistance,* 59.
117. Brown and Maclean, *Human Rights,* 200.
118. Vogelgesang, *American Dreams,* 88.
119. Kommers and Loescher, *Human Rights,* 232.
120. *Ibid.,* 236.
121. Brown and Maclean, *Human Rights,* 26.
122. *Ibid.,* 16.
123. *Human Rights in . . .,* 30.
124. Frankel, *Human Rights,* 19.
125. *Ibid.,* 18.
126. *Ibid.,* 27.
127. *Ibid.,* 128.
128. Gimlin, *U.S. Foreign Policy,* 8-9.

129. Forsythe, "American Foreign Policy," 37.
130. *Ibid.*, 50.
131. Thompson, *Moral Imperatives*, 64.
132. *The New York Times*, 22 July 1977, A 4, 6.
133. Address to the American Bar Association, March, 1978.
134. *Foreign Assistance*, 11.
135. Vogelgesang, *American Dreams*, 149-50.
136. Thompson, *Moral Imperatives*, 62.
137. Mower, *United States*, 141.
138. *Ibid.*
139. Thompson, *Moral Imperatives*, 59.
140. *Foreign Assistance*, 67.
141. Brown and Maclean, *Human Rights*, 67.
142. Sandra Vogelgesang, "What Price Principle?" *Foreign Affairs* 56 (July, 1978): 839.
143. Gimlin, *U.S. Foreign Policy*, 10.
144. Frankel, *Human Rights*, 43. Frankel, late professor of international law at Columbia University, even goes so far as to say that "so long as rights are rights, they are priority items on the public agenda, they lie outside the range of everyday political decisions." 44.
145. *Ibid.*, 43.
146. Thompson, *Moral Imperatives*, 15-16.
147. *Ibid.*, 13.
148. Brown and Maclean, *Human Rights*, 106.
149. Vogelgesang, *American Dreams*, 67.
150. Mower, *United States*, 125.
151. *Foreign Assistance*, 4.
152. Ved P. Nanda et al. *Global Human Rights* (Boulder, CO: Westview, 1981), 70.
153. Frankel, *Human Rights*, 5.
154. Kommers and Loescher, *Human Rights*, 224.
155. *Foreign Assistance*, 75.
156. *Ibid.*, 5.
157. *Ibid.*, 30-31.
158. *Foreign Assistance*, 27, 29.
159. Kommers and Loescher, *Human Rights*, 220.
160. *Foreign Assistance*, 92.
161. *Ibid.*, 80.
162. *Ibid.*
163. *Ibid.*, 34-35.
164. *Ibid.*, 81.

165. *Ibid.*, 77.
166. *Ibid.*, 83.
167. Nanda, *Global Human Rights*, 23.
168. Donald M. Fraser and John P. Salzberg, "Foreign Policy and Effective Strategies for Human Rights," *Universal Human Rights* 1 (January-March 1979): 13.
169. Brown and Maclean, *Human Rights*, 153.
170. Forsythe, "American Foreign Policy," 45.
171. John M. Goshko, "After Derian Leaves State, Whither Human Rights Policy?" *Washington Post*, 8 February 1981: A3.
172. Richard Cohen, "Abandoning the Quality that Makes Us Better," *Washington Post*, 2 December 1980: C1.
173. Rights Champion Reagan?" *Christian Science Monitor*, 5 May 1981: 28.
174. *Country Reports on Human Rights Practices for 1981*, a report submitted to the Committee on Foreign Affairs, U.S. House of Reps. and the Committee on Foreign Relations, U.S. Senate by the Department of State, 97th Cong., 2nd Session (2 February 1982), 9. Hereafter simply *Country Reports.*
175. *Human Rights and U.S. Policy in the Multilateral Development Banks*, hearings before the Subcommittee on International Development Institutions and Finance of the Committee on Banking, Finance and Urban Affairs, House of Reps., 97th Cong., 1st Session (21,23 July 1981), 35.
176. *Nomination of Ernest W. Lefever*, hearings before the Committee on Foreign Relations, U.S. Senate, 97th Cong., 1st Session (18, 19 May, 4 and 5 June 1981), 215. Hereafter simply *Lefever Nomination.*
177. *Country Reports*, 4.
178. *Ibid.*, 5.
179. *Ibid.*, 8.
180. Jeane J. Kirkpatrick, "East/ West Relations: Toward a New Definition of a Dialogue," *World Affairs*, v. 144, 1 (Summer 1981): 26-27.
181. For this see especially the President's speech before the British Paliament, "Promoting Democracy and Peace," *Current Policy* #399, 8 June 1982, U.S. Dept. of State, Bureau of Public Affairs.
182. *Country Reports*, 8.
183. *Ibid.*
184. *Lefever Nomination*, 147.

185. "Two Kinds of Human Rights?" 18 July 1981, *Washington Post:* A20.

186. Elliott Abrams, "Human Rights and the Refugee Crisis," *Current Policy* #401, 2 June 1982, U.S. Department of State, Bureau of Public Affairs.

187. Among the recently released document on this subject are: *Patterns of International Terrorism:* 1980 (PA 81-10163u June 1981), a research paper prepared by the CIA: Amb. Anthony C. E. Quainton, *The Challenge of Terrorism: the 1980s.* U.S. Department of State, Bureau of Public Affairs, *Current Policy* #230; *Review of the Presidential Certification of Nicaragua's Connection to Terrorism,* a hearing before the Subcommittee on Inter-American Affairs of the Committee on Foreign Affairs, House of Reps. 96th Cong., 2nd Session (30 September 1980: and Thomas O. Enders, *Cuban Support for Terrorism and Insurgency in the Western Hemisphere,* U.S. Department of State, Bureau of Public Affairs, 12 March 1982, Current Policy #376.

188. *Country Reports,* 9.

189. "Kirkpatrick Assails Rights Action," *Washington Post,* 25 November 1981: A6.

190. Jeane J. Kirkpatrick, "Human Rights and the Foundations of American Democracy," *World Affairs,* v. 144, 3 (Winter 1981/82): 198.

191. *Country Reports,* 2.

192. Richard Allen, "For the Record," *Washington Post,* June 1981: A18.

193. *Ibid.*

194. Kirkpatrick, "Foundations of Democracy,": 198.

195. Allen, "For the Record,": A18.

196. Michael Novak and Richard Schifter, "Speeches before the United Nations Commission on Human Rights, *World Affairs,* v. 143, 3 (Winter 1980/81): 242-43.

197. *Ibid.,* 243.

198. *Country Reports,* 6.

199. *U.S. Policy in the Multilateral Development Banks,* 46.

200. "Excerpts from State Department Memo on Human Rights," *New York Times,* 5 November 1981: 5.

201. *Country Reports,* 2.

202. Novak and Schifter, "Speeches," 248-49.

203. *U.S. Policy in the Multilateral Development Banks,* p. 29.

204. "OAS General Assembly Meets in St. Lucia," *Department of State Bulletin,* v. 82, 205 (January 1982): 2.

205. *Country Reports,* 9.

206. Elliott Abrams, "Human Rights Situation in El Salvador," *Department of State Bulletin,* v. 82, 2061 (April 1982): 37.

207. Abrams, "Refugee Crisis,": 2.

208. *Lefever Nomination,* 9.

209. *Country Reports,* 11.

210. *U.S. Policy in the Multilateral Development Banks,* p, 30.

211. Abrams, "El Salvador,": 68.

212. Abrams, "Refugee Crisis,": 2.

213. *U.S. Policy in the Multilateral Development Banks,* p. 34.

214. *Lefever Nomination,* 273.

215. *Country Reports,* 10.

216. Jeane J. Kirkpatrick, "Establishing a Viable Human Rights Policy," *World Affairs,* v. 143 (Spring 1981): 334.

217. Novak and Schifter, "Speeches," 231.

218. *Country Reports,* 10 and Ronald Reagan, "Promoting Democracy and Peace."

219. *Lefever Nomination,* 2.

220. Warren Christopher, "For the Record," *Washington Post,* 14 August 1980: A18.

221. Reagan, "Promoting Democracy and Peace,": 4.

222. Ferdinand Mount, "What is a Proper Human Rights Policy?" *Wall Street Journal,* 23 June 1981: 32.

223. Jeane J. Kirkpatrick, "Why not Abolish Ignorance?" *National Review,* 9 July 1982: 829.

SELECTED BIBLIOGRAPHY

Articles:

Abrams, Elliott."Human Rights and the Refugee Crisis." *Current Policy* # 401, 2 June 1982, U.S. Department of State, Bureau of Public Affairs.

_____ . "Human Rights Situation in Nicaragua." *Department of State Bulletin,* v. 82, # 2061, April 1982: 69-71.

_____ . "Human Rights Situation in EI Salvador." *Department of State Bulletin,* v. 82, # 2061, April 1982: 68-69.

Allen, Richard. "For the Record." *The Washington Post,* 4 June 1981: A 18.

Arnold, Hugh M. "Henry Kissinger and Human Rights." *Universal Human Rights,* v. 2(October-December 1980): 57-71.

Bonker, Don. "Human Rights: Will Reagan Learn from Congress?" *The Christian Science Monitor,* 7 January 1981: 23.

del Carril, Mario. "Signals From State." *The Washington Post,* 10 February 1981: A 14.

Cohen, Richard. "Abandoning the Quality that Makes us Better." *The Washington Post.* 2 December 1980: C 1.

Derian, Patricia M. "Human Rights and American Foreign Policy." *Universal Human Rights,* v. 1(January-March 1979): 3-9.

"Excerpts from State Department Memeo on Human Rights." *The New York Times*, 5 November 1981:

Fageen, Patricia Weiss. "The United States and International Human Rights, 1946-1977." *Universal Human Rights*, v.2 (July-September 1980): 19-33.

Forsythe, David P. "American Foreign Policy and Human Rights." *Universal Human Rights*, v.2(July-September 1980): 35-53.

Forsythe David P. and Wiseberg, Laurie S. "Human Rights Protection: A Research Agenda." *Universal Human Rights*, v. 1(October-December1979): 1-24.

Fraser, Donald M. and Salzberg, John P. "Foreign Policy and Effective Strategies for Human Rights." *Universal Human Rights*, v. 1(January-March 1979): 11-18.

Gersham, Carl. "The New Totalitarianism: Soviet Oppression." *World Affairs*, v. 144, # 3(Winter 1981/82): 214-20.

Geyelin, Philip. "Human Rights Turnaround." *The Washington Post*, 12 December 1980: A 23.

Goshko, John M. "After Derian Leaves State, Whither Human Rights Policy?" *The Washington Post*, 17 January 1981: A 3.

"Human Rights Choice Abhors Scolding as U.S. Tool." *The New York Times*, 13 February 1901: 2.

"Interview with Walter Cronkite (Excerpts)." *Department of State Bulletin*, v. 81, # 2049, April 1981: 10-11.

Johnson, M. Glenn. "Historical Perspectives on Human Rights and U.S. Foreign Policy." *Universal Human Rights*, v. 2 (July-September 1980): 1-18.

Kirkpatrick, Jeane J. "Dictatorships and Double Standards." Commentary, v. 68, 5(November 1979): 34-35.

_____ . East/West Relations: Toward a New Definition of a Dialogue. *World Affairs*, v. 144, 1(Summer 1981): 14-30.

_____ . "Establishing a Viable Human Rights Policy." *World Affairs,* v. 143, 4(Spring 1981): 323-34.

_____ . "Human Rights and the Foundations of Democracy." *World Affairs,* v. 144, 3(Winter 1981/82): 196-203.

_____ . "Why Not Abolish Ignorance?" *National Review,* 9 July 1982: 829-31.

"Kirkpatrick Assails Rights Action." *The Washington Post,* 25 November 1981: A 6.

Kristol, Irving. "The Common Sense of 'Human Rights'." *The Wall Street Journal,* 8 April 1981:

_____ . "The Timerman Affair." *The Wall Street Journal* 29 May 1981: 24.

Lefever Ernest W. "The Trivialization of Human Rights." *Policy Review* 3(Winter 1978): 11-26.

"Making Trouble on Human Rights." *The New York Times,* 30 November 1981: A 18.

Mohr, Charles. "Coalition Assails Reagan's Choice for State Department Human Rights Job." *The New York Times,* 25 February 1981: 10.

Mount, Ferdinand. "What is a Proper Human Rights Policy?" *The Wall Street Journal,* 24 March 1981: 34.

Novak, Michael. "The Reagan Approach to Human Rights Policy." *The Wall Street Journal,* 28 April 1981:

Novak Michael and Schifter, Richard. "Speeches Before the United Nations Commission on Human Rights." *World Affairs,* v. 143, 3(Winter 1980/81): 226-64.

"OAS General Assembly Meeting." *Department of State Bulletin,* v. 82, # 2058, January 1982: 1-9.

Oberdorfer, Don. "Across-Board Rights Policy Adopted." *The Washington Post,* 6 November 1981: A 14.

Olsen, Edward A. "How to Keep Human Rights Alive Under Reagan." *The Christian Science Monitor,* 11 August 1981: 23.

Reagan, Ronald. "Promoting Democracy and Peace." *Current Policy* # 399, 8 June 1982, U.S. Department of State, Bureau of Public Affairs.

"Reagan Rights Report: Slight Shift in Emphasis." *The Washington Post.* 8 February 1982: A 1.

"Rights Champion Reagan?" *The Christian Science Monitor.* 5 May 1981: 28.

Safire, William. "Human Rights Victory." *The New York Times,* 5 November 1981: A 27.

Seabury, Paul. "Disraeli, Gladstone and the Human Rights Debate." *The Wall Street Journal,* 23 June 1981: 32.

"Second Try on Human Rights." *The Washington Post,* 6 November 1981: A 30.

"Two Kinds of Human Rights." *The Washington Post,* 6 November: A 30.

Vogelgesang, Sandra. "What Price Principle?" *Foreign Affairs,* 56(July 1978): 819-41.

"Wrong Turn on Human Rights." *The New York Times,* 6 February 1981: 22.

Books:

Braham, Randolph, ed. *Human Rights: Contemporary Domestic and International Issues and Conflicts.* New York: Irvington, 1980.

Brown, Peter G. and Maclean, Douglas, eds. *Human Rights and U.S. Foreign Policy: Principles and Applications.* Lexington, Mass.: Lexington Books, 1979.

Farer, Tom J. *Toward a Humanitarian Diplomacy: A Primer for Policy.* New York: New York University, 1980.

Frankel, Charles. *Human Rights and Foreign Policy.* Headline Series 241, October 1978. New York: Foreign Policy Association.

Gimlin, Hoyt. *U.S. Foreign Policy: Future Directions.* Editorial Research Reports. Washington, D.C.: Congressional Quarterly, 1979.

Human Rights: A Symposium. Proceedings of the General Education Seminar, volume 6, number 2, Columbia University. New York: University Committee on General Education, 1978.

Human Rights in United States and United Kingdom Foreign Policy: A Colloquium. Held at the Palace of Westminster, November 27-28, 1978.New York: American Association for the International Commission of Jurists, 1979.

Kirkpatrick, Jeane J. *Dictatorships and Double Standards— Rationalism and Reason in Politics.* New York: American Enterprise Institute, Simon and Schuster, 1982.

Kommers, Donald P. and Loescher, Gilbert D., eds. *Human Rights and American Foreign Policy.* Notre Dame, Ind.: Univ. of Notre Dame, 1979.

Mower, Alfred Glenn. *The United States, the United Nations, and Human Rights: the Eleanor Roosevelt and Jimmy Carter Eras.* Westport, Conn.: Greenwood Press, 1979.

Nanda, Ved P. et al. *Human Rights: Public Policies, Comparative Measures, and NGO Strategies.* Boulder, CO: Westview, 1981.

Ramcharan, B. G. *Human Rights: Thirty Years After the Universal Declaration.* The Hague: Martinus Nijhoff, 1979.

Rubin, Barry M. and Spiro, Elizabeth P., eds. *Human Rights and U.S. Foreign Policy.* Boulder, CO: Westview, 1979.

Thompson, Kenneth W. *The Moral Imperative of Human Rights: A World Survey.* Washington, D.C.: Univ. Press of America, 1980.

Vogelgesang, Sandy. *American Dreams, Global Nightmares: the Dilemma of U.S. Human Rights Policy. New York: Norton, 1980.*

Government Publications:

Country Reports on Human Rights Practices for 1981. A report submitted to the Comm. on Foreign Affairs, U.S. House of Reps. and the Comm. on Foreign Relations, U.S. Senate by the Department of State, 97th Cong., 2nd Session (February 1982).

Human Rights and U.S. Foreign Policy. Hearings before the Subcommittee on International Organizations of the Comm. on Foreign Affairs, 96th Cong., 1st Session (May 2, 10; June 21; July 12; and August 2, 1979).

Human Rights and U.S. Foreign Assistance: Experiences and Issues in Policy Implementation. A report prepared for the Committee on Foreign Relations, U.S. Senate, by the Congressional Research Service, Library of Congress, 96th Cong., 1st Session (November, 1979).

Human Rights and U.S. Policy in the Multilateral Development Banks. Hearings before the Subcomm. on International Development Institutions and Finance of the Comm. on Banking, Finance and Urban Affairs, House of Rep., 97th Cong., 1st Session (21, 23 July 1981).

Human Rights in Eastern Europe and the Soviet Union. Hearings and Markup before the Comm. on Foreign Affairs, 96th Cong., 2nd Session (16, 24 September, 1980).

Nomination of Ernest W. Lefever. Hearings before the Comm. on Foreign Relations, U.S. Senate, 97th Cong., 1st Session, on nomination of Ernest W. Lefever, to be Assistant Secretary of State for Human Rights and Humanitarian Affairs (19, 18 May, 4, 5 June 1981).

Resolution of Inquiry Concerning Human Rights Policies. Hearing before the Comm. on Foreign Affairs, U.S. House of Reps., 96th Cong., 2nd Session (16, 24 September 1980).

The American Values Projected Abroad Series

Western Heritage and American Values: Law, Theology and History
Alberto Coll

Political Traditions and Contemporary Problems
Edited by *Kenneth W. Thompson*

Institutions for Projecting American Values Abroad
Edited by *Kenneth W. Thompson*

Essays on Lincoln's Faith and Politics
Hans J. Morgenthau and David Hein
Edited by *Kenneth W. Thompson*

The Predicament of Human Rights: The Carter and Reagan Policies
Nicolai N. Petro
With a preface and introduction by *Kenneth W. Thompson*

Writing History and Making Policy: The Cold War, Vietnam, and Revisionism
Richard Melanson

American Diplomatic Traditions and Values: The Founders
Edited by *Norman Graebner*

American Diplomatic Traditions and Values: 1840-1940
Edited by *Norman Graebner*

American Diplomatic Traditions and Values: The Postwar Era
Edited by *Kenneth W. Thompson*

0-8191-3326-4